Deborah Groves

Deborah Groves is a specialist neurodivergent acting coach, arts accessibility coach and creative enabler, working with dyslexic, dyspraxic, ADHD and ADD stage and screen actors, writers and dancers. She develops strategies, based on an individual's strengths, to overcome their challenges, and sets goals to improve their creative work life, their working practice and their wellbeing.

Deborah is dyslexic and dyspraxic, which she discovered when she was in her forties. Her sessions and workshops use this personal understanding and her compensatory strategies, plus years of experience studying and working with neurodivergent creatives.

She began her career as a classical singer studying at the Guildhall School of Music and Drama, and moved to classical actor training at LAMDA and RADA. She has a Master's degree in Applied Theatre Education from the Royal Central School of Speech and Drama and is a qualified postgraduate one-to-one tutor of neurodivergent learners in higher education, and a member of the accredited body, The Professional Association of Specific Learning Difference Specialists in Higher Education.

She sang in opera choruses, and produced and performed with a charitable opera company for many years. She also works as a freelance specialist in film and theatre, and has been involved in projects at Chicken Shed Theatre, the Royal Court, the Almeida, Shakespeare's Globe, the Royal Shakespeare Company, and for Paramount Pictures, Netflix and accredited drama schools throughout the UK.

'A staggering achievement. Deborah is amazing! If you're a dyslexic actor (or not), it's all in this book!' *Tolú Fagbayi*

'You will find this book a life-changer. Being dyslexic means you have gifts – so read about them here. A fantastic book (and audiobook) to learn from.' *Lloyd Everitt*

'An actor never knows where to start, but at last there is a guide for how to do it. Deborah's process is clear and brilliant. I have developed my craft around this work – and so will you.' *Joshua Griffin*

'Deborah knows how to play and how to have fun in a safe space, but at the same time develop the best work you are capable of making.' *Billy McCleary*

'Deborah has taught me so much. I cannot tell you what an expert she is about acting and being dyslexic. Read (or listen) to this book. Now I have a reliable craft, and my first pro job was at the Globe!'
Tanika Yearwood

'I've worked with Deborah since I was fifteen – and finally got to drama school. She understands what it is to be dyslexic. The great exercises in the book will grow inside you over time to become the most fantastic toolbox.'
Paige Charlton

'The strategies here are "slay"!' *Rakhee Sharma*

Deborah Groves

The Dyslexic Actor's Toolkit

Strategies for Success in Your Craft and Career

NICK HERN BOOKS
London
www.nickhernbooks.co.uk

A Nick Hern Book

The Dyslexic Actor's Toolkit
first published in Great Britain in 2025
by Nick Hern Books Limited,
The Glasshouse, 49a Goldhawk Road,
London W12 8QP

Copyright © 2025 Deborah Groves
Illustrations copyright © 2025 Oliver Brooks

Deborah Groves has asserted her moral right to be identified as the author of this work

Designed and typeset by Nick Hern Books
Printed and bound in Great Britain by SRP Ltd, Exeter

A CIP catalogue record for this book is available from the British Library

ISBN 978 1 84842 660 3

www.nickhernbooks.co.uk/environmental-policy

Nick Hern Books' authorised representative in the EU is Easy Access System Europe – Mustamäe tee 50, 10621 Tallinn, Estonia *email* gpsr.requests@easproject.com

For
Paige, Rakhee, Rachel, Joshua,
Mac, Tanika, Hummy, Phoebe, Frey-Frey
and Margaret and Colin Groves

Contents

Foreword ix

Introduction 1
   What is dyslexia? 3
   Other forms of neurodivergence 10
   How to use this book 13

Part One: You 17
   Identity 17
   For actor training and rehearsals: How you learn 26

Part Two: Your Skills 33
   Voice 33
      Preparing your voice 34
      Accents 42
      Singing 47
   Movement 55
      Preparing your body 56
      Dance 64
      Combat and intimacy 68
      Character movement and physicality 71

Text 79
    Research 80
    Understanding the text 90
    Navigating the play 108
    Getting to know your character 115
    Bringing the lines to life 126

Shakespeare 134
    Structure 138
    Language 147
    Character 154

Sight-reading 165
Line-absorbing 171

Part Three: Your Career 193

Auditioning 193
    Planning for the audition 194
    Working on the audition material 204
    On the day... and beyond 210

Rehearsals 217
Wellbeing 225
Time management and organisation 248
Finances 271

Afterword: Supporting the Dyslexic Actor 282

Acknowledgements 291

A note from the publisher

We are determined that this book is as accessible as possible for all readers.

In designing the layout, we have closely followed the British Dyslexia Association's Dyslexia Style Guide regarding the size and style of font, spacing and structure, headings, colour, paper and other visual aspects. You can read more at:
bdadyslexia.org.uk/advice

However, we know that neurodivergent people have a wide variety of access requirements, so we have also made the book available in audio and digital formats. There is also accompanying video content to illustrate techniques described in the book.

If you have other requirements to make this book accessible for you, please email us at:
access@nickhernbooks.co.uk

Foreword

I found out in my forties that I wasn't stupid after all. This was thanks to my dear friend Kara Tointon's TV programme, *Don't Call Me Stupid*. After many years of assuming I was, a professional assessment confirmed that I was dyslexic and dyspraxic. Many confusions fell into place, and now I could start to get to know myself and my true identity in this new liberated and somewhat scary form.

I believed the only way to test that I wasn't stupid was to attempt a Master's degree, and clutching onto three GCSEs from thirty years ago, I studied Applied Theatre Education at the Royal Central School of Speech and Drama. It was at this point that I realised I really wasn't stupid; in fact, I found I had an insatiable thirst for learning, and a commitment to it.

Thanks to support from the Neurodivergent Department and the fabulous course leader, my life gradually transformed to a brighter, technicolour world of curiosity and discovery. I became addicted to experimenting more and widening my academic knowledge in order to become a specialist in neurodivergent people and their place in the arts world.

But what could I do with this learning? My desire was to offer a practical acting guide to the millions who think they are 'stupid' or different from others – in or out of the arts – so they wouldn't struggle like I had. My positionality as a white, female, lesbian, middle-class, educated, dyslexic dyspraxic is that of privilege. I was afforded a lot of advantage in my life and yet I felt at a constant disadvantage. If I did, then so must many others.

I was not taught how to learn, how to remember, how to revise for exams, how to sight-sing… and this led to shutting down my entire educational experience. For the global majority, their positionality often has far less advantage. With this intersectionality in mind, I wanted my thoughts and strategies to be available for everyone to try to access an acting craft, whatever their positionality.

Introduction

'What you can do, or dream you can, begin it.
Boldness has genius, power and magic in it.'
Goethe, *Faust* (trans. John Anster)

So you are an actor, or want to be – and you're dyslexic, or think you might be.

Dyslexic people are amongst the most amazing, colourful, fun, humorous, intelligent, successful people in the world. Determined, unyielding, versatile, pioneering, instinctive, spontaneous, exceptional, brilliant and creative.

However, there is something paradoxical about being dyslexic. On the one hand you function brilliantly, you may overachieve at certain things and impress others. And yet on the other hand you notice you have difficulties, are self-doubting and fearful, and struggle with a shame that you feel you're not quite good enough.

In this book I will try to do what I feel dyslexic people want: take something complicated and offer it to you more simply, to make sure every part of any process is understood. I will also attempt to show you how to do things in a way that will make your life easier. Over time, as you become more curious and confident, you can add more layers and become the expert in yourself, your learning and your craft.

The Dyslexic Actor

During my time working with actors and trainees, the same questions and remarks have arisen time and time again. Some of them are thoughts all actors have, but all of them have been raised by the dyslexic people I have worked with:

- 'My bad memory scares me.'
- 'Why don't I process information properly?'
- 'Huh, my disorganisation...'
- 'My total lack of confidence...'
- 'I never give my best at a casting because my sight-reading/line-learning lets me down.'
- 'I drive the director mad. I'm so slow to know what's going on.'
- 'I think I may have some sort of dyslexia because I can't understand sequences and repeat them.'
- 'I just don't get voice sessions – I feel nothing I'm meant to feel. I can't even do simple sound exercises.'
- 'I'm asked what I think in a read-through and I don't know what I think – and if I do feel something, I can't put it into words.'
- 'Can you help me understand what's going on?'

Along with the above, the most common challenges shared to some extent or other among the dyslexic creative people I work with are:

- Understanding their identity and feeling authentic in their sense of self
- Knowing how they think and learn best
- Time management and organisation

- Sight-reading
- Line-learning
- Text analysis
- Tackling Shakespeare
- Mental and physical wellbeing
- Movement
- Vocal warm-ups
- Being understood/supported by other actors, tutors, agents, casting directors, directors.

You are not alone in feeling these frustrations and I believe that over time you will come to be more aware of your strengths and gifts and use them to overcome some of your challenges in a more balanced way. Hopefully this book will go some way towards offering strategies for you to access your craft more effectively and confidently.

Over time you will realise there is no 'normal':

> **'Normal is nothing more than a cycle on a washing machine.'**
> Whoopi Goldberg

What is dyslexia?

Dyslexia's literal meaning suggests that it is 'a difficulty with reading, writing and spelling'. 'Dys' is from the Greek word meaning 'difficulty', and 'lexia' is from the Greek word meaning 'word'. Whilst that can be part of it, however, it's so much more.

Being dyslexic is a way of life that can be brilliant,

painful, fun, quirky, spectacular, frustrating, weird and extraordinary. It's a way of being and, in my opinion, is not something you 'have', it is who you *are*.

Dyslexia presents different challenges, feelings, emotions and strengths for everyone. It is not a typical way of learning or being. It has been known about for over a hundred years, but is still widely misunderstood, and varies from person to person. Interestingly, dyslexia is often accompanied by other neurodivergent elements of brain difference.

Some dyslexia facts

- A dyslexic person tends to show a disparity (a difference) between intelligence and the ability to communicate it
- Dyslexia is genetic: from birth
- It is passed through families
- It doesn't go away
- It varies in form from person to person, both in strength and intensity
- It comes with gifts and strengths, and offers amazing possibilities for wonderful achievements
- It can make you feel stupid or inadequate, especially in learning environments
- It does not need medication
- Many dyslexics are not identified (diagnosed) until adulthood.

If you are dyslexic, you might notice challenges with:

- Understanding what you are hearing
- Understanding what you are reading
- Processing, keeping hold of and remembering information
- Reading without stumbling
- Recognising and working out individual sounds that make up words
- Spelling
- Putting thoughts into spoken words
- Finding the word that's on the tip of your tongue
- Telling left from right
- Dealing with alterations to a schedule or arrangement
- Focusing and concentrating
- Working alone.

You might also find that you tend to:
- Make mistakes
- Muddle similar words
- Have to re-read the same paragraph several times
- Feel easily confused, or overwhelmed
- Feel misunderstood
- Feel different in a way that others might regard positively as 'a quirky uniqueness', but is embarrassing to you.

It is important to remember that this long list is of 'commonalities' (common things), some of which you may notice apply to you, and some of which don't.

One particularly interesting aspect to consider can be a fluctuating sense of self – where one moment you feel confident, motivated and driven to achieve absolutely anything, and the next you feel like your self-esteem is dramatically plummeting: you have no resilience, you feel useless, exhausted, confused, disorientated and misunderstood.

Now let's remember that dyslexia also comes with incredible gifts, strengths and positive super-powers. Across the page are just a handful of examples of world-famous achievers who are, were or were likely to have been dyslexic.

Strengths associated with being dyslexic

There is good news: you will have immeasurable strengths that will enable you to learn to achieve and fulfil your dreams.

Strengths, or gifts, associated with dyslexia are:
- Being innovative
- Being creative
- Strong communication skills
- Being determined and driven – seeing a goal and wanting to achieve it
- Being energetic
- Being observant
- Curiosity and awareness about all that is around you
- Being highly intuitive
- Making a strong team player
- Being empathetic
- Being imaginative
- Being a good listener

Introduction

- Being emotionally intelligent – understanding your own and others' emotions
- Being able to clearly see the whole picture
- Being able to use your body to express what you can't say
- Being able to turn problems into creative solutions
- Having strong interpersonal skills
- Being obsessively hard-working to achieve your goals
- Being good at visualising things
- Being practical
- Being able to watch, learn, feel and manoeuvre with great skill
- Being able to find places through instinct
- Being highly tuned to remember environments, events, and important personal experiences, and associate information to these occasions
- Being good at seeing patterns
- Being able to align similarities and differences/ imbalances and disparities
- Being able to take things apart and rebuild them
- Having out-of-the-ordinary thinking
- Being very quick and humorous
- Being able to delegate.

As we have acknowledged, we are all individual, but these strengths are frequently seen in dyslexic people, and you may notice some of them yourself.

Why would a person who is dyslexic want to act?

Why would you, a dyslexic person, want to read script after script and perform in front of people, if you struggle with words and text, embarrassment, anxiety, a see-sawing sense of self, and low self-esteem and confidence? Surely you'd be crazy to even consider it?

The answer's easy! The strengths you may notice as a dyslexic person are absolutely what is needed to act. I see it time and time again. Being able to play, to react to what you are hearing, to listen, engage, imagine, empathise and transform; to be intuitive, emotionally available, active, energetic, committed, determined, spontaneous, courageous and a big-picture thinker; to break rules, have a desire for fairness and truth, an ability to build relationships and to understand humanity – are just what is needed to be a fine actor!

Plus, you're used to:
- Having to put more work in than a neurotypical person
- Being afraid
- Making mistakes
- Being thrown into uncomfortable situations or put on the spot
- Finding courage from somewhere
- Thinking outside the box
- Solving problems
- Following a creative vision
- Wanting to find the truth, potentially after many years of pretending

- Dreaming and being determined to achieve a long-term goal.

Other forms of neurodivergence

Other forms of neurodivergence include dyspraxia or Developmental Coordination Disorder (DCD), Attention Deficit (Hyperactivity) Syndrome (ADHD), dyscalculia, dysgraphia and Autism Spectrum Condition (ASC).

You can research and learn more about yourself from this Neurodiversity Umbrella:

This book is not designed to address each of these others in detail, but we will look a little at dyspraxia below, as it is currently identified as part of assessments for dyslexia, and the two regularly co-occur, and share features.

You might have sprinklings of some of these neurodivergencies, along with the various strengths that can accompany them. Many of the strategies included throughout the book will be of use *whatever* your neurodivergency.

What is dyspraxia?

Dyspraxia is also known as Developmental Coordination Disorder (DCD). It manifests as a challenge with co-ordination and cognition. This includes how we develop knowledge and understanding through learning. It has no formal method of identification of its own, so it is currently identified as part of the dyslexia identification assessment.

Whereas a dyslexic person can often think visually, with a good 'visual sketchpad' in their minds of what to do, a dyspraxic individual can't necessarily visualise the order to put things in in their mind. All the many things to do are frantically flashing through the brain but can't be put in an order. This impacts the organisation of everything, and in particular, time management.

It can also be associated with unusual things like balance and feeling disorientated whilst moving. You may be clumsy, easily become dizzy or travel sick, be accident prone, forgetful or disorganised, and you may not have been well coordinated as a child.

A performer with dyspraxia may have challenges with:
- Day-to-day organisation
- Learning new information
- Telling left from right
- Memory
- Coordination
- Throwing and catching

- Dancing
- Remembering dance or movement sequences
- Finding places and following directions
- Map-reading.

You may also find that you tend to:
- Feel confused, or overwhelmed
- Feel awkward, or clumsy
- Look at words on the page and recognise them but not be able to find their meaning in your head
- Start a statement and then forget what you are talking about
- Go off on tangents
- Be outspoken or direct
- Speak too loudly at times
- Stand too close to others.

You may have done very well at school, and you may enjoy reading, and taking in information, but can't keep hold of it.

I work with many dyspraxic actors who overcome all of the above challenges because they:
- Are highly motivated
- Practise
- Receive support and training.

They are bright, intelligent and well coordinated because they are aware of, and determined to overcome, their dyspraxic challenges.

How to use this book

This book is designed so that you start by getting to know yourself, then you will look closely at the core skills an actor needs, then some of the practicalities of a career in performance. Finally there is a chapter that is written for non-dyslexic people who are working with you. It's designed to guide them through how best to support you. You can read it for your own understanding, and you can share ideas from it with other people, to help them to help you.

Every reader should read Part One: You. After that, if you like, you can just check the contents page and jump to the section you need help with right now.

The book is structured around Goals, Obstacles and Strategies. For each key idea I will clearly state the goal you are trying to reach, then list and explain some of the things that stand in the way, and finally present some practical strategies to help you overcome those obstacles and achieve the goal.

This book also has its own online resources, where you will find lots of links to sources of further information about dyslexia, some creative inspiration, and some helpful tools to support you. Sometimes, an idea in the book is demonstrated in a video online.

You'll know when you see this symbol:

To find all the links and videos, visit:
www.nickhernbooks.co.uk/dat-resources

The Dyslexic Actor

Here's a short exercise to show you that when it comes to creativity, there is no right or wrong. And it's intended to be fun!

Grab a pen/pencil, and set a timer for one minute. Then turn each circle on these pages into something – for example, a flower, a face, the sun…

Go!

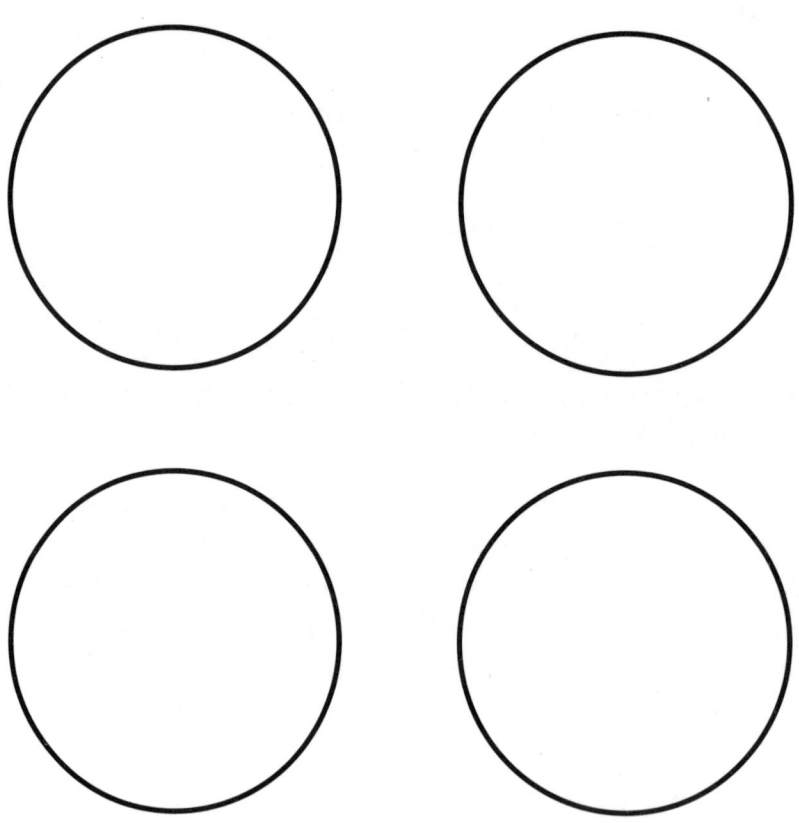

Introduction

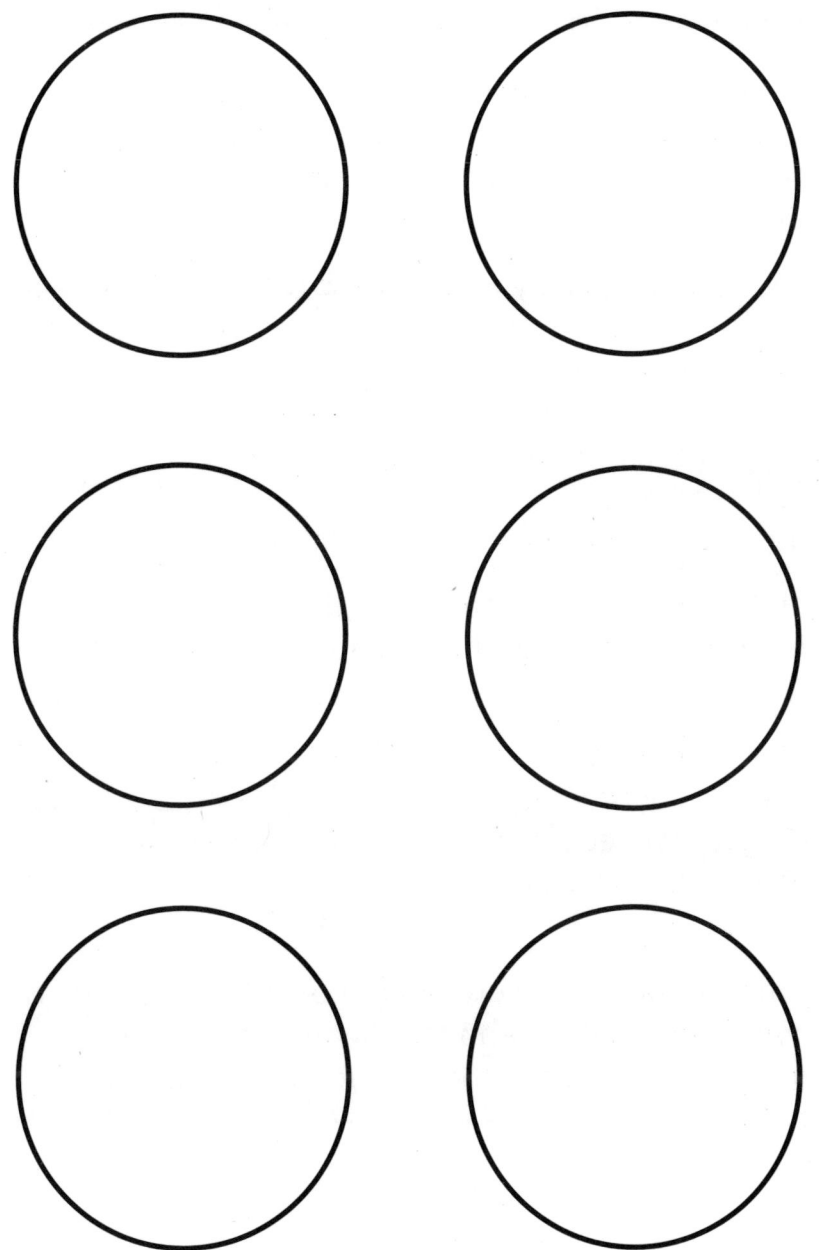

How did you do? Did you find creative uses for each circle?

The point of this game is to give an example of how you should approach your craft. This is play. It is not something to be feared, because there is no right or wrong.

Acting, like the game you just played:
- Requires intense focus: having a purpose and working on an objective
- Uses imagination
- Is goal-orientated
- Is based on fun
- Is a way of developing knowledge.

When I refer to 'play' in this book, I don't mean it frivolously, I mean that there is no right or wrong!

- Playful focus
- Playful creativity
- Playful spontaneity
- Playful reflection
- Playful knowledge
- Playful learning!

Play also shows and allows you to be different. You are *unique* and *individual*. And that is one of your biggest strengths. Never forget that this is *vital* in your acting craft. Vital!

Part One: You

Identity

Whatever happened to you in the past, it's only a fraction of your life. You determine your future, your past does not. You can choose to be what you want. Some of you will have left school without knowing how you learn best. Not until you understand yourself and how you learn will you be able to help others train or direct and understand you.

Many people I meet have only recently been identified with a learning difference. This can produce all sorts of feelings very personal to the individual. Some find it a revelation and release; others are sad, angry or bitter. It can take several months, if not years, to adjust to the new self you discover. It's really important to understand who *you* are before you can possibly consider inhabiting the character of another person as an actor.

- Have you ever looked at who you are? (your identity)
- What characteristics make you *you*?
- Do you feel authentic? (i.e. genuine, not a 'copy' of someone else)

If you have spent years conforming to a schooling system that didn't or doesn't work for you, you may have had to alter who you are to fit in. Have you tried to be what you are not? If so, you will have a misguided view of who you are.

In order to train or rehearse effectively and communicate in a team, you have to know your authentic self. Find a way to be accepting, informed and feel ok about who *you* are.

Being dyslexic is misunderstood. It can be a real nuisance for the person training or directing you, and endlessly frustrating being you. Unless you know yourself, and are able to talk openly about how you best respond to instruction, no one else will know how to support you. I hope the strategies here, although simple, will support you to discover your identity.

> YOU need to become the expert on yourself to help others understand you.

Every dyslexic person is different. This is why it's important to spend time peeling back the layers and thinking about how you work. When you have a better understanding of all the amazing characteristics that make you unique, and the defences you put up when you feel unsafe and vulnerable, you will have a more balanced outlook on yourself, and you'll be able to work much more effectively. Now is the time to take ownership of being a neurodivergent person of distinction.

Part One: You

Goals and obstacles

Goals
- To discover the positive, best version of yourself, based on your personal and creative achievements to date
- To become authentic and at ease – living the truest expression of who you are.

Obstacles
All actors can suffer with a sense of not being 'good enough', however, the neurodivergent actors I work with often have particular challenges with:

- A wobbling wave of worry
- Feeling overwhelmed
- A swinging sense of self esteem that soars high

19

> at certain times and plummets to the ground at others
> - A spiky profile of success and disasters that surges up and down, down and up
> - A never-ending circle of success and failure, confidence and crisis
> - Lack of knowledge of their own strengths.

Here are some strategies to help you overcome these obstacles and achieve your goals.

Strategies

1. Identity box

What is it?
This is a box where you keep all sorts of information about yourself and your identity.

Why is it useful?
It is devoted just to you, and it keeps you organised. Everything is together in the same safe place, so you know where to find it.

How do I do it?
Find an old shoe box and decorate it however you want, with images of things you love, or fun stickers or colours. Alternatively, go out and buy one.

Put the box somewhere easily accessible where you won't lose it. On your desk or under your bed, for example.

To start with, fill it with important documents and all sorts of information personal to you: passport, certificates, driving license or copy, reports, diplomas, reviews, any printed CVs or headshots, etc.

As you work your way through the strategies on the following pages, also place what you create in the box.

2. Achievements list

What is it?
In this strategy you detail all your achievements; all the things that make you you. It gives you time to sit and consider what you have achieved.

Why is it useful?
Your achievements list reminds you of your factual worth. Whenever you're feeling down, just take a look at this list and it will help remind you that you're special – and often more talented than you feel.

How do I do it?
Take a pen and some paper and write all your achievements down. They could be anything and everything. For example:

- I passed my cycling proficiency test aged eleven
- I saved up and travelled around the world for six months
- I raised £500 for MIND
- I passed my driving test
- I arranged a party for all students at the end of term

- I passed my Grade 3 piano exam
- I played the role of ......
- I sew and make my own clothes.

Now put this list in your Identity Box, and if you're feeling down and in need of a boost, take a look.

3. Jelly person

What is it?
Drawing a big jelly person outline and filling it with all your strengths.

Why is it useful?
The jelly person is a useful reminder of your positive attributes. You might find it easier to list your weaknesses, but you do have talent and many fantastic skills, so don't be shy to think about them.

How do I do it?
Sketch a big blobby jelly person. Fill the jelly person with the strengths that you can genuinely own as part of your identity.

Store the sketch in your Identity Box as a reminder of your strengths and attributes.

4. Jelly person's friends

What is it?
This image focuses on your strengths *and* areas you could improve on.

Why is it useful?
It allows you to see your strengths and areas for improvement clearly, which can help you gain a clearer understanding of yourself and the areas which you need to work on.

How do I do it?
Ask five people you trust:
- One word to describe you best
- What they think your greatest achievement is
- One thing you could change for your own benefit
- What they value most about you
- Your three greatest strengths.

Now take another piece of paper and draw you as a jelly person. Draw five jelly friends around the outside. Now write down in each of those jelly friends the answers that person gave to the questions you asked.

In your own jelly person, in the middle, try to summarise the answers that come up most often; that best represent you.

Place your jelly self and friends in your Identity Box.

5. Honest heart

What is it?
The honest heart is an exercise to help you reflect on what's going on deep down inside: your defences, and how they might stop you achieving your goals.

When others come to you with a problem, are you able to clearly see their dilemma from the outside and throw some light on the situation? If only that were true of yourself! This exercise allows you to do just that.

Why is it useful?
As you move forward with your training or work as an actor, the voice in your head that you live with should be acknowledged, but only ever as a positive encourager, like a friend, with trust in you.

It's so easy for this voice to slip into negative thoughts; 'I'm not good enough', 'I did that wrong', 'everyone else is better than me'. This is not good for your mental health or your professional development. This voice needs to have a determined mindset: there is endless proof that positive thinking creates positive results.

Having identified your defensive and obstructive thoughts, you can notice them when they creep in, and seek to eradicate them.

How do I do it?
Draw a big heart on a plain piece of paper. Fill the heart in with your vulnerabilities. Be honest. For example:

Part One: You

Now reflect: what might be stopping you succeeding in your next goal? Look at what you've written, as well as one thing that someone told you in the Jelly person's friends exercise (page 23) that you could consider trying to change for your own benefit. Set out some strategies for yourself to follow.

For example:

- From now on if I don't understand an instruction or exercise, I shall stop guessing and say so. I deserve clarity.

Place the Honest heart findings in your Identity Box.

For actor training and rehearsals: How you learn

> 'Education is not the learning of facts,
> but the training of the mind to think.'
> Albert Einstein

In both actor training and professional rehearsals, you will be taking in new information while working as part of a group, because teamwork is an essential part of the profession. However, some of that group, and the director/facilitator, may not be dyslexic like you.

If you don't know how you learn, you will not get the most from any training or rehearsal process. Now that you have a clearer sense of your identity as a dyslexic person, your next task is to work out how you learn best.

Dyslexic minds thrive on information being:
- Simple
- Clear
- Logical
- Structured
- Easy to understand and follow.

The process of learning and practising the craft of acting is:
- Complex
- Time-consuming
- Multi-layered
- Analytical

- Open to many interpretations
- Not right or wrong.

So how do you deal with this?

Prepare yourself to listen and absorb. In any group situation, you are unlikely to get the gist of what you are learning from one neurotypical way shown to you. Armed with the knowledge of *how* you will learn best, you can help yourself, and also help the director to support you.

Goal and obstacles

Goal
To learn information in a way that works for you.

Obstacles
- Being given any one-method approach to learning, e.g. 'Just read the play.'
- The speed at which information is given to you verbally
- Failure to check in on what you have learned as you go along.

Strategy

The layered multi-sensory process

A neurodivergent person will most often learn best by applying a layered, multi-sensory process. This means:

Layered
1. Work out what your *goal* is: the point of the thing you are trying to learn.
2. Gather *small chunks of information*, with time to process:
   - Set yourself reasonable timeframes in which to do each layer, e.g. 'I'll do this for an hour', so that each task feels manageable and you don't run out of time to do everything
   - Do one after the other (layering the information)
   - Reflect on how that layer was for your learning
   - Repeat the step again if you would like to
   - Move to the next step or layer.

Multi-sensory
When you are gathering the small chunks of information, you should do so using several of your senses:
- *Look* at information (read or watch)
- *Hear* the information (audio)
- *Touch/visit* (where possible) something tangible.

Even taste and smell can be useful for some learning processes!

Using more than one sense applies to how you *gather* the information, and also how you *capture* it for yourself. So you may want to write notes, and/or draw pictures, and/or take photos, and/or make recordings, etc.

The secret is that all of these ways, layered up, add to a nice deep overall understanding.

An example

Let's imagine that you have the opportunity to attend a general meeting with a casting director or a director. They want to meet you, engage and interact with you, but this is not an audition – there is no script to prepare or knowledge of a piece of work to build on. You need to have something to say, so though this might be very difficult and daunting for you, you need to learn or accumulate information for discussion.

Let's say the person you're going to meet is Sir Richard Eyre – world-acclaimed director of film, TV, theatre and opera. The best place to start is by finding out 'who is he?' and 'what has he done?'.

You need to be a detective.

The Dyslexic Actor

Goals
1. To find out about Sir Richard. What he does, his type of films, theatre, opera. Any recent works, any projects on the go.
2. To prepare some questions to ask him, or statements you can confidently make about something of his you enjoyed.

Layer 1

(Remember to give yourself a specific chunk of time for this task.)

Look at information about Richard and his works.

- Read articles
- Watch interviews on YouTube
- Read or watch plays or films he has directed.

Capture key information: Write down interesting bullet points, do a mind-map or drawings. Even if you're just writing words, use different colours to make the ideas visual.

Reflect. How well do you feel you understand so far?

Layer 2

(Remember to give yourself a specific chunk of time for this task.)

Hear about Sir Richard and his work and life in audio interviews from the radio, or podcasts. Think about where the best environment is for you to do this – would you take the information in better if you listen

Part One: You

to it while going for a walk, or sitting somewhere quiet at home?

Capture key information: If you don't yet know how best you learn, try using a different method of capture to the one you used in Layer 1.

Reflect. How well do you feel you understand so far?

Layer 3

Touch/visit something tangible. Sir Richard was the Artistic Director of the National Theatre in London for twelve years. If you can, go to the theatre. If you can't, don't worry, skip to Layer 4 for a different sensory learning approach.

Capture key information: If you go to the National Theatre, you could take photographs or video to remind you of the place (but not during a play!).

Reflect. How well do you feel you understand so far?

Layer 4

Speak into a recorder or camera what you have retained about Sir Richard.

Reflect. Do you now have any questions to ask him, based on all you know? For example:
- With such a varied directing and writing career – is there anything you are keen to do in the future?
- Do you like to take on projects that have relevance to your life?

31

- What has been most rewarding of all your projects?
- How do you like to run a rehearsal room?
- Have you any advice for an actor like myself wanting to be proactive?

Repeat any of the layers to satisfy your curiosity.

Now that you know a little more about yourself and how you learn, we can move on to some of the practical skills of being an actor – the challenges they can present, and some strategies to overcome those challenges.

> **Don't forget:**
> Whatever you are trying to learn, to understand, or to master, a layered, multi-sensory approach to doing it will support you best of all.

Part Two: Your Skills

In this chapter we will work through each of the key skills that an actor needs to develop, and identify the challenges which arise for dyslexic actors in honing these skills. Then we'll work through strategies which might help you to address these challenges.

There are sections on:
- Voice
- Movement
- Text
- Shakespeare
- Sight reading
- Line-learning

Voice

Your voice is one of your most precious tools as an actor. You are recognised by it. It allows you to express yourself and also your character. You need to train your voice so you have the strength and versatility to project in a theatre, as well the ability to play with pitch, tone and accents.

Voice will be covered in your actor training, however this can be a challenging area for dyslexic actors who need clear and simple instructions. Sometimes it's hard to understand the way you are taught, and important bits of information are lost.

Further resources for help with voice work

This chapter contains a simple warm-up for your voice; and a layered, multi-sensory and practical approach to learning accents, and to singing.

For more detail, a number of highly-respected practitioners have offered excellent techniques to explore voice work:

- Cicely Berry
- David and Rebecca Carey
- Barbara Houseman
- Kristin Linklater
- Jeannette Nelson
- Patsy Rodenburg

Buy one of their books, look at some of their online videos, or, if you are able to, take a class.

Preparing your voice

- What is your current voice practice like?
- Do you nurture and exercise your voice as much as your body, or less?

- Do you do voice work on a regular basis? For example, do you work on flexibility, resonance, clarity and tone?

Don't underestimate the need for regular voice work. Your voice must serve you well. Musicians and athletes practise, practise, practise: drilling, repeating and focusing to increase their endurance. It's a good idea to develop your own straightforward voice warm-up that you can use again and again as an independent actor. The strategies in this section add up to outline an easy warm-up for you which comprises the essential parts of voice work.

Goals and obstacles

Goal
To be able to warm up your voice safely, and knowing that this warm-up covers everything that is needed.

Obstacles
Being afraid that you're not doing it correctly or well enough, or you're missing elements out.

Strategies

Warming up your voice should comprise six stages. They are:

1. Warming up your body/stretching
2. Increasing breath flow
3. Engaging your diaphragm

4. Warming up your face/articulators
5. Building resonance
6. Articulation

1. Warming up your body/stretching  A

What is it?
Stretching your neck, spine, hips and muscles.

Why is it useful?
It wakes you up, gets the blood flowing and allows for your voice to travel through your body without you carrying excess tension.

How do I do it?
- Start by doing the cat-cow yoga pose: From a position on all fours on the floor, drop your pelvis low so that your belly hangs towards the floor, then slowly reverse the position, with the movement travelling up your spine so that your back is arched up towards the ceiling. Gradually return to your starting position with your belly hanging down and your chest pushing forward, and so on. Repeat 5 times.

- Now, stand in a neutral pose, with your feet planted firmly hip-width apart, and your knees soft – not locked back. Stretch your neck by tipping your head to one side, then lift the arm

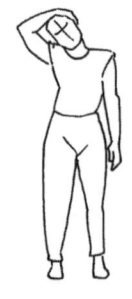

on the side you are leaning your head towards, and place your hand on the side of your head. Allow the weight of your arm to stretch out your neck, without pressing down hard on it – you don't want to damage your neck. Hold for 10 seconds. Repeat on the other side.
- Return to your neutral pose, look straight ahead, and drop your head down. Allow the weight of your head to stretch the back of your neck. For an increased stretch, place your hands on the back of your head, and without pulling down hard, allow the weight of your arms to stretch your neck. Hold for 10 seconds.
- Move your hips in a circle in one direction starting small and getting bigger. Now repeat in the opposite direction.
- Circle your ankles, hands and shoulders in one direction and then the other, starting with small circles and allowing them to grow increasingly larger.
- Stretch out any other parts of your body that feel stiff and in need of a stretch.

2. Increasing breath flow  B

What is it?
Encouraging you to breathe deeply, expand your ribcage and take in more air.

Why is it useful?
Breathing deeply calms and centres you. Working on your breath capacity also helps you sustain longer lines of text at greater volume, and connect more deeply to what you're saying.

How do I do it?
- Squat with your bum hanging low to the floor and your spine curved. Take in deep breaths right down into your diaphragm. Imagine that you're breathing from your bum. Feel your back inflating and deflating as you do this.
- Now stand with your legs hip-width apart, and knees slightly bent. Raise your arms into the air and pull one arm with your hand across to the other side, bending like a banana. You should feel a deep stretch down that side. Breathe deeply into the stretched side for three breaths. Repeat on the other side.

3. Engaging your diaphragm  C

What is it?
An exercise to help you find and engage your diaphragm.

Why is it useful?
Your diaphragm is what gives your voice support. It allows you to speak and shout at greater volume safely, without damaging your vocal folds.

How do I do it?
- Put one hand under your belly button and the other

on your side. Cough. Do you feel your lower belly and side move? That thing that is moving is your diaphragm.

- Now make some unvocalised punchy sounds: 'sh' 'pf' 'ss'. Punch them out. Feel your diaphragm engage. Repeat for 5 rounds.

4. Warming up your face/articulators

 D

What is it?
Waking up your eyes and ears and loosening your jaw, tongue and lips.

Why is it useful?
Warming up your face helps you form words and sounds faster and more precisely.

How do I do it?
- Imagine you're chewing a very small toffee. Keep chewing, and allow that imaginary toffee to grow until it takes up your whole mouth and you have to use your entire face to chew it.
- Yawn, and use your hands to pull down your face as you do so, stretching out your jaw.
- Find the gristly bit of muscle that connects your top and bottom jaw, just by your ears. Give it a good massage for 10 seconds.
- Clean your teeth with your tongue, going round 8 times one way, and then 8 times the other. Make sure you get to those teeth right at the back too!

- Pout your mouth like Paris Hilton then smile a big wide smile. Repeat 10 times.

5. Building resonance  E

What is it?
Allowing the sound you make to travel through your body so it resonates and projects more powerfully.

Why is it useful?
Having a good resonant voice means the audience can hear you more clearly and you have to do less work vocally. This also means you're less likely to tire out your voice or damage your vocal folds.

How do I do it?
- Start with a gentle humming. Push the sound forward from your diaphragm (not your throat!) so that your lips are buzzing and tingling.
- Now take another breath, hum again and this time direct the sound into your chest. While you do this, beat your chest like Tarzan.
- Repeat again, this time sending the sound into your nose and forehead.
- You can do this for as long as you want. You should start to feel your body vibrating and tingling as you hum.

6. Articulation  F

What is it?
Exercises to wake up your tongue and teeth.

Why is it useful?
Articulation is getting your words out clearly, cleanly and crisply, without stumbling. Improving your articulation with exercises means that you'll be heard and understood by the audience.

How do I do it?
Have a go at these tongue twisters:

- Peter Piper picked a peck of pickled peppers
  A peck of pickled peppers Peter Piper picked
  If Peter Piper picked a peck of pickled peppers
  Where's the peck of pickled peppers Peter Piper picked?

- Betty bought a bit of butter
  But she found the butter bitter
  So she bought a bit of better butter
  To make the bitter butter better

- She sells seashells on the sea shore
  The shells she sells are seashells I'm sure

- The sick sheik's sheep's sick (repeat over and over)

- Red lorry, yellow lorry (repeat over and over)

Start saying the words slowly. Really get your mouth around the sounds. If you keep getting it wrong, start again and go slower. As you practise the tongue twisters you will become better and better, and be able to go faster and faster, warming up your mouth to work.

Accents

At some point you are bound to audition for or play a role that will require you to learn an accent that isn't your own. It's an important part of your versatility to be able to do other regional or national accents of English.

For this reason, accent and dialect work is a standard part of actor-training. However, the methods used to learn accents in drama schools can be challenging for dyslexic actors, rather than playing to their strengths.

> ### Goals and obstacles
>
> **Goal**
> To feel confident to offer an accent as needed for a role.
>
> **Obstacles**
> Theoretical learning models such as the 'International Phonetic Alphabet' (IPA), and vowel sounds in the 'kit list'. More often than not, these approaches are unhelpful for dyslexic actors who need a more practical, multi-sensory model.

Strategies

The key for dyslexic actors is to think practically about embodying the accent. Using the actor's often finely attuned ear to impersonate, and improvise, and practise, and adding powers of observation to notice how the accent is formed in the mouth of the speaker.

Try out the following strategies and see what works for you.

1. Hear the musicality of the accent

What is it?
Listening to the melody an accent makes, and learning to imitate just the shape of the tune at first.

Why is it useful?
Some accents sound quite flat, using a small pitch-range, others are spoken with a great variety of inflection – getting an accent right is not only about the pronunciation of words but also about the variation of pitch.

How do I do it?
Listen to a native speaker, in real life or using the International Dialects of English Archive (IDEA): www.dialectsarchive.com

Notice the musicality of the accent. What is its pattern, its shape or its tune? Where and how much does the melody of the accent go up and down? Can you listen to and re-create just the melody, without the words at first?

2. Observe the physicality of the accent

What is it?
Experimenting with how the accent feels in your mouth.

Why is it useful?
It's a practical approach which makes use of your powers of observation.

How do I do it?

Find a video of someone speaking in the accent, online. YouTube videos are good because you can select the option to slow the video down, BUT, be careful what you choose: it's always best to find a native speaker rather than someone 'doing' the accent.

By stopping and starting the video, try to copy individual phrases.

While doing this, notice the general shape the accent makes in the mouth, and how it differs to your natural accent. How do you have to adapt your mouth-shape to make the same sounds? Does the accent feel wide in your mouth compared to your own? Or high? Is it vertical? Does it roll around your mouth like a ball?

For example:

- Is a Scottish accent wider and flatter than your own? If so, lean in to that to help you find the accent: imagine your mouth is the shape of a rectangle, and think about your lips stretching sideways as you speak.
- Is a New York accent harder work for your jaw than your own? Do you have to open your mouth wider to make the same sounds? What if you imagine your mouth as a washing machine and roll the words round and round your mouth?
- Are the vowels in an RP (Received Pronunciation) accent more open than your own? If so, see what happens if you think of your mouth as having a ruler placed in it vertically. Imagine opening your mouth at

the dentist: 'ahhhh'. Or perhaps they're actually more closed? Then imagine your jaw is held together with elastic and control that urge to open wide.

Now look in more detail at the way in which the accent's speaker forms their vowel sounds – A, E, I, O, U. What shape does the mouth adopt for each of these? Is it more open, or narrower than in your native accent?

Finally, notice how consonants are formed. 'R' and 'L' are often big ones to change from accent to accent, so you could start by looking out for those. How does the placement of the speaker's articulators – their tongue, lips, and teeth, differ from yours?

3. Try using a trigger sentence  G

What is it?
Using a trigger sentence to help you get into an accent.

Why is it useful?
Often a phrase that we associate with an accent sticks in our mind. Saying the phrase aloud can help you slip easily into the rhythms, sounds and musicality of the accent, and can set your mouth in the right shape ready for speaking other words and phrases.

How do I do it?
Have a go at saying these phrases in these accents:

- Australian – 'Why don't you come to Australia and try the beef pies?'
- Northern Irish – 'How now brown cow' / 'Eiderdown'.

- Welsh – 'Malvolio is wearing yellow stockings.'
- General American – 'Sam's an American writer who takes vitamins.'
- Newcastle – 'Jean Paul Gaultier got his finger stuck in a photocopier.'

Do you slip naturally into each accent from these phrases? Now make up your own. Think about sounds and phrases you associate with a particular accent, and remember them for whenever you need a key into that accent.

4. Practise in real-life situations

What is it?
Striking up a conversation in the accent you are learning.

Why is it useful?
It is one thing to practise alone, it is another to have the courage to communicate using the accent. This requires respect, being prepared to get it wrong, working out ways of improving, and practising. Whether you tell the person you are speaking to that you are practising for a role, or you keep it to yourself – it works!

How do I do it?
Be inventive and playful! Order coffee or food in a café using the accent. Make a telephone call, an enquiry. Visit a DIY store to ask how something works. Chat to the assistant in a department store.

If you have access to a native speaker of the accent, or are able to immerse yourself in the accent's home environment by going to the place where it is spoken, this strategy is even better, though it's extra-important to practise with respect for those whose accent you are mimicking.

Singing

Many dyslexic people have a fantastically strong musical ear, and are confident singers, although, like neurotypical people, there is a whole spectrum of ability and not everyone would describe themselves as a singer. However, actors are often asked to sing, even in productions which are not 'musicals' – and singing comes into actor training for everyone too.

> ### Goals and obstacles
> **Goal**
> To enjoy performing and offer a committed delivery to the audience.
>
> **Obstacles**
>
> - You can't read music.
> - You feel self-conscious singing.

Strategies

Pavarotti didn't read music. Dame Judi Dench would never call herself a singer, but if you look up a video of her singing, what an example she is of commitment to the text and to her intention. Singing is just another form of communication – another reason to react. So don't panic, and consider some of the strategies below to see if any are useful.

1. Reframe your mindset

Set your mind to 'It is not about me'.

Set your mind to 'I don't have to have a wonderful vocal instrument'.

Set your mind to 'I am only the vessel of communication'.

Remember it is your body through which the composer's intention is transported to the audience. No one is interested in you.

So take 'yourself' out of the equation and focus on:

- The composer, who wrote the music
- The lyricist, who wrote words that form your *intention*, the *reason* you must sing
- The audience, who need to know *why* you are singing.

If you are singing a song as yourself, (not a character in a play), all of this is even more important. Feeling self-conscious is natural, but your mindset needs to be focussed on the information you are giving and not the person you are.

Let me explain:

If the building you are in is on fire and people are asleep in their homes, you need to bang on the doors and get everyone's attention.

'Get out of the building!' you shout.

At the bottom of the stairs when you've called the fire brigade, everyone is assembled and you need to tell them what to do:

'Leave the building quickly! The building is dangerous, it may explode and collapse. Run as far away as possible to safety.'

What is your intention here?

What obstacle do you have to get over?

Are you interested in how you look or sound as you give the instructions?

There is a cost to you and to everyone involved if you do not get your intention across.

This is what is needed when singing.

Relay the important information and use your intention.

It must matter, and the audience must understand what is going on.

Sing as if your life depends on it.

2. Familiarise yourself with the song

Tune

Read the music if you can, and if not, don't de-stabilise yourself by thinking you are less of a performer. You just do it differently, and it can be just as effective. With notes, rhythms, length of notes, words and accompaniment, there is a lot going on to overwhelm a dyslexic mind. Your job, as always, is to take the complicated and make it simple.

Do one process at a time, layered on top of each other:

1. Listen to several different versions of the song. What do you feel/see in your mind's eye? Colours, atmospheres, rhythms? Note down how it feels to you.
2. Is your song accompanied by one instrument or several? What atmosphere does the accompaniment give you? What do you notice about your vocal line on top? Do they work together in partnership or are they conflicting? The accompaniment is like the sea on which a boat travels, and you are the boat going along on top of the accompaniment. A valuable partnership.
3. Play the song on your instrument if you can.

Rhythm

Can you feel a heartbeat, or a rhythm? Tap this rhythm, or walk to the rhythm that feels right to you. Embody the tune into your physicality by playing it repeatedly as you move around the room to the song. Many dyslexic people have a musical ear that can pick up tunes and embody them with tremendous competence.

Pitch

What do you notice about the pitch: the highs and the lows of the song? As you listen, stand tall for the higher moments, crouch low for the lower moments.

Do you feel like an animal moving in the space? Or a piece of material flowing in a breeze? Notice what the movement of the song means to you.

3. Research – know your narrative

What is the narrative (story) you are telling?

For an example, look online for the lyrics to the following song:

> 'So In Love', from *Kiss Me Kate* (based on *The Taming of the Shrew*, by William Shakespeare), composer: Cole Porter.

The research needed for a song is just like that for a monologue. The song comes at a particular place in the musical and for a particular reason.

1. Research the musical, opera, or musical play that the song comes from. Do all the detective text analysis

work that you would do for a play. (There is a lot more on this subject starting from page 79.)
2. Research the composer and lyricist for interesting facts and other works they may have written. Do any of your findings give clues that relate to this musical piece?
3. Research your character based on what is said about you in the musical and what you say about others.
4. Study the text before you sing and decide why you are singing what you are singing. What are you reacting to that has prompted you to begin?
5. What is your intention when you are singing? (In the Cole Porter example, perhaps it is 'I need to persuade them that I love them'.)
6. Speak the words as dialogue. Reflect on what you have said out loud. Does this help to form your intention?
7. What obstacle do you need to get over? – (Perhaps in this example 'I must overcome my pride, my worry I may be rejected'.)
8. Go through the text of your song. Mark in your breaths at the end of every thought.
9. What is the feeling inside you that makes you say (or in this case, sing) the next thought?
10. Write out each thought in your own words.
11. Underline the verbs in a colour of your choice to show you the 'action' of the song. Verbs are 'doing' words that make action happen. What do the different verbs show you is happening in the song?

12. Remember, songs often repeat the same words again and again in a way that wouldn't be natural in dialogue. Take time to consider that each repetition is a different thought and needs to be delivered to the audience differently each time: 'So in love... So in love... So in love with you, my love, am I.'

4. Explore the written music (only if you would like to)

If you can read music, or are curious about how it looks on the page, look at it for an overall big picture as you listen to the music. Sheet music can be confusing, so don't do anything that feels overwhelming.

1. There is pitch: how high or low the notes are as they go up and down. If anything surprises you in the up and downs, mark it.
2. There is rhythm that makes up the heartbeat of the music. Rhythm is made up of note-lengths – whether they are long or short. What do you notice about this? Is there anything to highlight that takes you by surprise or helps you?
3. There is the setting of words – the lyrics – against the notes. Do you notice any particular words that are sung more slowly or fast? Does this make them more important, or less? Does the music give you space for breaths which follow the thought, or do you have to break the thoughts to breathe? Try, if you can, to sing the song both ways – does it sound better to put breaths in which follow the thoughts, or which follow the music?

4. There are dynamics – louds and softs – which are marked on the music in a sort of code. As the language of musical notation is most commonly Italian, 'forte' or 'f' means loud, and 'piano' or 'p' means quiet.

fff	very very loud
ff	or 'fortissimo' – very loud
f	or 'forte' – loud
mf	or 'mezzo-forte' – medium loud
mp	or 'mezzo-piano' – medium soft
p	or 'piano' – soft
pp	or 'pianissimo'– very soft
ppp	very very soft
<	or 'crescendo' – gradually louder
>	or 'diminuendo' – gradually softer
sfz	or 'sforzando' suddenly loud, with emphasis

5. Finally, consider the accompaniment beneath your vocal line. What do you notice about the instrument(s) supporting you? Does it fill in gaps when you don't sing? Does it play louder or softer than you, or follow your dynamics?

All of these layers may help with your understanding of the song you are singing, and your ability to convey the thoughts and intention of the song to the audience.

Movement

Movement is an essential, exciting and valuable part of being an actor. However, dyslexic and dyspraxic actors required to move, dance, and fight often despair with frustration. They feel overwhelmed, process slowly, don't grasp steps, get left behind in sequences and muddle left and right.

The fact is, movement training and rehearsal may be challenging, but you can compensate for this with the correct mindset, determination and hard work.

You will learn movement by:
- Modelling – *seeing* demonstrations of what you're trying to learn
- Repetition
- Practising little and often
- Using multiple senses.

One tip I would offer if you would like to do general work on your body and your movement skills, is to attend regular ballet classes.

You don't have to aspire to be a ballerina, or have the physique of a ballet dancer, to do this. Ballet will help you to find your core (the centre of your alignment) and improve your balance. It allows you to focus completely on your body and connect with each different part of it in a slow, methodical way. It develops your consciousness of your own body in the space and involves coordinated exercises between your arms and legs, and it also builds strength and muscle memory.

See if there are any local classes you can go to. It's much better to be in the room with a teacher than doing it online.

Preparing the body

A physical movement warm-up is important as part of everyday life for an actor, in and out of training. Dyslexic actors often ask if there are example movement warm-ups to follow – something short, but effective.

> ## Goals and obstacles
> **Goal**
> To be able to warm up your body safely, and knowing that this warm-up covers everything that is needed.
>
> **Obstacles**
> Being afraid that you're not doing it correctly or well enough, or you're missing elements out.

Strategies

Here is a body warm-up divided into four manageable chunks, although really the whole thing flows into one 15-minute warm-up:

Part Two: Your Skills

1. Centring
2. Extensions and release
3. Rotations and the inner expressive world
4. Connecting with the Earth

The set-up

This is a short physical warm-up to be used before a first-round audition or self-tape. If the audition requires rigorous physical activity, physical ensemble work, or dance, use this as a 'pre-' warm-up, before engaging the body in a longer more specific warm-up tailored to what you are about to do.

Find a private space where you can extend the full reach of your limbs. Ensure you feel comfortable to close your eyes or to take a soft gaze in this space. This may be an audition breakout space, your living room, or a quiet park.

All movement offers are suggestions, they are open to adaptation and translation to encompass the uniqueness of all bodies. There is no one way to move. Work to where your body is comfortable and celebrate your uniqueness as your greatest power.

1. Centring  H

1. Place one hand on your belly button and one hand on the side of your ribs. As you breathe in, visualise your hands filling with air. As you breathe out, the air pours back out of your palms. Repeat 4 times.

2. Grip your toes into the ground and release. Repeat 4 times.
3. Work across your toes, peeling them away from the ground and then pressing each toe into the ground.
4. Rock forward and back through your feet. Enjoy the moment when you are just about to come off balance. Repeat 4 times.

Then continue into...

2. Extension and release

5. Reach up and pull down a long piece of imaginary rope, hanging from above. Alternate your arms and think about reaching to the full extension, and then pulling down into the centre of the body. At the same time, explore treading through the feet, as if squelching through mud.

6. Place your feet wider than your hips, in a diagonal position so the toes point out to the space. The rope has transformed, and now there is a giant bell on the end of it. Reach your arms out and up, and with both hands, pull the rope down into the centre of the body, ringing the bell. At the same time bend through your knees, sending them over the toes. Connect

the ringing of the bell to your exhale of breath. Repeat 4 times.
7. Reach up with both hands, extending the arms above the head, thinking about lifting up – up – up towards the sky. Then lower one arm and curve the other arm over your head, so the torso is curved to the side like a banana.

8. Tap lightly along your rib cage and connect it to a long vowel sound that you make vocally.
9. Release your torso, following the spine all the way down, so you hang towards the floor, like a puppet released from its strings. Try not to lock your knees, bend them very softly instead.

10. Gently swing from one side to the other, releasing your head and creating space in the jaw.
11. Bend your knees, send the tailbone down to the floor, and roll your spine back up to standing. Visualise each vertebra of the spine reeling back on top of the one below it, until the head arrives, bringing your focus back out to the world.
12. Repeat from step 7 on the other side, curving your 'banana' to the opposite side to the one you did before. It may help to pick items from the space, e.g 'my first time I will curve over towards

the door. The second time I will curve over to the window.'

13. After you have swung from side to side as in step 10, imagine you have paint on your shoulder blades, and by rotating them you can draw a figure of 8.
14. Bend your knees, send your tailbone down to the floor, and spinal roll back up to standing.

Then go on to...

3. Rotations and the Inner Expressive World  J

15. Place your feet in a soft parallel under your hips. Close your eyes or take a soft gaze. Imagine that just in front of your face is a floating piece of silk. On the exhale of breath, gently press your face into the silk, releasing the jaw, the muscles behind your eyes and all of the muscles in your face.
16. Gently open your eyes, and leaving one foot flat on the floor, come onto the ball of the other foot. Imagine inside your ankle joint there is honey, and by rotating the joint the honey warms up. Rotate 4 times in each direction, then switch to the other foot.
17. Progress up through the body, rotating the knees, the hips, and the spine 4 times each way, warming the honey.

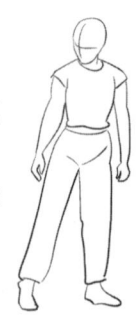

18. Place your eyeline onto your shoulder, rotate your shoulder backwards and forwards 4 times, warming the honey.
19. Bring your hand to your shoulder, lift your arm and place your eyeline on your elbow. Now try to draw the perfect circle with your elbow.
20. Extend your arm down by your side, place your eyes on your fingertips, draw a huge circle next to you with your arm fully extended. Rotate the arm forwards and back 4 times. Enjoy each fall of your arm and connect this to your exhale breath. Also explore if you can bend your knees at the same time as each fall of your arm, then straighten them as the arm goes back up.
21. Repeat the circular arm sequence on the other side.
22. Close your hands into a fist. Starting from the thumb, peel each finger open to a wide position, stretching through the palm. Rotate the wrists. Close the hands into a fist and peel each finger open again. Repeat 4 times.
23. Imagine in between your hands is a fizzing ball of energy, like a mini sun with a mind of its own. This shifts your body from one side to the other. Keep following this fizzing ball of energy as if it is trying to show you this space for the first time from a

new perspective. It may speed up, or slow down, perhaps it wiggles in and out, circles you around, lifts you up and all the way down to the floor.

24. Imagine you can take the fizzing ball of energy and place it next to your heart. Feel it joining with the rhythm of your heartbeat and spreading across the body.

Then move on to...

4. Progression: Connecting with the Earth  K

25. Send both arms up above your head. Then, starting from the fingertips like a candle melting, release the arms down, and bring the forehead down towards the centre of the chest. Spinal roll all the way down to the ground at the pace that works for your body today.
26. When you reach the ground, put your knees down, and pad your hands out on the floor so that you move into a tabletop position. Place your hands under your shoulders, your knees under your hips.
27. Bring your forehead in towards your belly button, rounding the spine towards the ceiling. Then shift the belly button to the floor and lift the chin towards the ceiling. Keep coming back to your breath leading the shift of the spine.

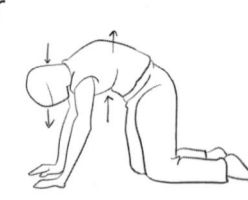

28. Inhale and tuck your toes under, then exhale as you lift your hips toward the ceiling, straightening your legs. Your body should form an inverted V shape. Keep your hands shoulder-width apart and press them firmly into the floor. Spread your fingers wide for stability. Engage your core and try to straighten your spine while keeping your head between your arms, looking back at your feet. Relax your neck and let your heels sink toward the floor. If your heels don't touch the ground, that's fine. Think about keeping a slight bend in the knees. Hold the position for around 4 breaths. Focus on lengthening your spine and pressing your chest toward your thighs. To release, bend your knees and return to the tabletop position.
29. Step one leg forward into a lunge position, if needed, your back knee can rest on the floor. Hold this position for 4 breaths and then repeat on the other side.
30. Return to a tabletop position, melt down onto one side of the hip, then pour the body all the way down to the ground and roll onto your back in a star position.
31. Breathe in and out as if sinking deeper into the earth.

32. Curl over into a foetal position.
33. Spread back out extending into your greatest star.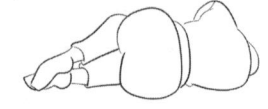
34. Then curl over again into a foetal position on the other side.
35. Gradually push yourself up to a seated position, as if you are peeling yourself away from your imprint in the earth. Take your time to pad your hands round and in towards your feet. Spinal roll all the way back up to standing.
36. Feel the floor beneath your feet, visualise the 360° space around you, like a glowing bubble.
37. Enjoy the unique rise and fall of your breath. Acknowledge the powerful connection to yourself and the exciting potential of welcoming in a character!

Dance

Dance is another skill which is often asked of actors even though they would not call themselves dancers, and it can present processing challenges for dyslexic and dyspraxic performers. As mentioned in the introduction to this section, regular ballet classes might help with some of this, but here are some strategies to help you if you are needing to learn a dance as part of your training or in rehearsals for a performance.

Goals and obstacles

Goal
To feel confident about learning a dance routine.

Obstacles
- Feeling overwhelmed by the speed of teaching
- Not having enough time to digest each section before moving on to the next
- Feeling disorientated.

Strategies

1. Coloured gloves and socks

What is it?
Having a different colour glove or sock for left and right.

Why is it useful?
It gives you a visual cue for left and right.

How do I do it?
When you are learning choreography, place different coloured socks and/or gloves on your left and right hands and feet. If you can, have the choreographer direct you using the colour instead of saying left or right. The choreographer may also be happy to wear those colours with you.

2. Speaking aloud the instructions given to you

What is it?
Speaking the instructions your choreographer gives you out loud.

Why is it useful?
Speaking the instructions aloud helps you process the information given to you as a rhyme or pattern. It can turn passive listening into active listening.

How do I do it?
After each instruction you're given, repeat it to yourself aloud and map it out with your body as you chant. If need be, ask the choreographer to repeat the instruction in smaller chunks. Repeat, repeat, repeat. Firm foundations allow you to move to the next stage.

3. Coloured signs on walls to signpost the geography of the piece

What is it?
Using colours as markers for where to move instead of directions like 'forwards' and 'backwards', 'left' and 'right'.

Why is it useful?
Moving towards a colour, instead of listening and translating an instruction into your body can make following the geography of dance moves much easier for a dyslexic or dyspraxic person.

How do I do it?
Put up different coloured posters on four sides of the

room. Get the choreographer to issue instructions in correspondence with the colours. For example, instead of saying 'move backwards', they should say 'move towards blue'.

4. Weighting certain parts of the body

What is it?
Using weights to weigh down certain parts of the body.

Why is it useful?
Dyspraxic people sometimes have the sensation that their body isn't connecting properly with the ground, and there can feel a lack of specificity to movement. Through weighing down parts of your body you can actually feel them, and connect with their movement, a lot more easily. This improves your brain's ability to figure out where different parts of your body are in the space.

How do I do it?
Tie mini weights to your wrists and ankles. Make sure the weights aren't too heavy, you still need to be able to move! You can buy bangle wrist and ankle weights online or you can improvise your own.

Now go through the steps of the dance/movement sequence you're trying to learn. As you move, you'll be able to feel your body much more, which will strengthen the connection between mind and body. You'll become more aware of the movements you need to make.

5. Filming the movement sequence

What is it?
A film you make of the choreographer and of yourself.

Why is it useful?
Filming the movement sequence will allow you to see a model of what is needed from the facilitator, so that you can see what your body should be doing, and compare it with what it *is* doing. Having your own visual guide to refer back to and practise in your own time is enormously helpful and will allow you to drill sections at home.

How do I do it?
Ideally, you would ask someone, or set up a fixed camera, to film you doing the movement sequence along with your choreographer – with you both in shot. This is best of all, because it will allow you to compare easily and to spot any mistakes you are making when you watch the video back.

When you watch it back, notice which bits you're getting wrong and which bits aren't in time, and work on them in little sections, practising over and over.

At home, break it down move by move, and keep drilling each move until it feels natural.

Combat and intimacy

As actors we are on occasion required to speak whilst following choreographed moves. The most common examples of this are in scenes with choreographed intimacy, and in stage combat – armed or unarmed.

As dyslexic actors, however, our mind and body can process information slowly and we can be overwhelmed by the amount of information being given to us at one time.

> ## Goals and obstacles
>
> ### Goal
> To learn choreographed movement which happens at the same time as dialogue without getting overwhelmed.
>
> ### Obstacles
>
> - Having too much information to process in one go
> - Trying to engage and learn with your brain and your body at the same time
> - Feeling under pressure to keep up with others' learning pace.

Strategy

One process at a time

What is it?
Breaking the work down into its separate processes and learning one at a time – not trying to do them all together straight away.

Why is it useful?
As we've seen throughout this book, the layering approach is the most important tip to remember. This is how dyslexic individuals learn best.

How do I do it?
Choose to learn the words first, or the moves first. It doesn't matter which.

If choosing to learn the words first, be sure they are embodied into you before you begin absorbing the moves. For tips on how to do this, turn to page 171.

When the words are fully embodied and come out automatically, start to learn the movement.

If you are being shown the movement pattern physically, to copy, be sure that the director/choreographer/facilitator is facing the same way as you and not mirroring you. They can stand at the side or in front of you and demonstrate the moves to be followed.

Repeat small chunks of information/moves slowly, again and again until you feel you can move on to the next step.

You may find that speaking the words you've learned while you learn the movement is useful straight away, so that you are learning to move on the line. However you may need to set the words aside once you've learned them, until the moves are really embedded in your body, and then bring them together.

Working with a partner/another actor on this process can seem embarrassing if they process faster than you. Take a moment to remember that in the arts we now work inclusively to embrace all people irrespective of any challenges they may have, and there is no need to apologise for slowing things down.

Character movement and physicality

No matter whether you are performing a monologue, mime piece, tableau, or scene with dialogue, your physicality is part of your actor's toolkit. Physicality, along with your voice and imagination, helps you to tell your story. It is important to develop your character's physicality, one that is very different from your own.

Finding out how to move as a character that is different from yourself can also be daunting. It can be difficult to access when our own way of moving is programmed within us. There are also some common strategies for actor movement which are taught in drama schools and favoured by directors but which can be confusing for some dyslexic actors – such as the work of Rudolf Laban. If this is the case for you, you may need to go along with it as best you can in class or in rehearsal, but have in mind some clear strategies which work for you and through which you know you can develop your character movement in your own time.

> **Goals and obstacles**
>
> **Goal**
> To be able to inhabit the physicality of a character different from your own.
>
> **Obstacles**
> The common use of methodologies which appear theoretical and complicated to the dyslexic actor, and put you in your head instead of in your body.

Strategies

1. Mine the text for your character's physical facts and history

What is it?
Relating your character research to its effects on the character's physicality.

Why is it useful?
The text is full of clues that do the job for you, if you can

dig them out they will help you to build a physical picture of the character.

How do I do it?
Turn to page 115 to find out about doing in-depth character analysis on the text. As part of understanding your character and their history, you will discover some clues about their physical state. Ask yourself some of the following questions to help you build their physicality:

- How old is your character? (A twelve-year-old, a fifty-year-old, and an eighty-year-old will all move differently.)
- How physically fit is your character? Are they strong or weak?
- Does their weight affect how they move? Do they move in a way that is unusual for their physical build (for example: a sprightly sumo wrestler)?
- What past or present physical challenges/ailments has your character had, if any? Injuries? Sickness? Pregnancy? How does that affect how they move?
- Does the character need assistance to move? Do they walk with a cane, crutch, walker, assistance animal, or a human assistant?
- Does the character even walk? Perhaps they crawl, creep, or roll (is your character even human? If it is some kind of supernatural being, then you have even more freedom to play.)
- Does the character's physicality change at any point? When? What causes the change? How does that affect the character?

2. Head to toe

What is it?
Using a clear, easy to follow process to develop your character's physicality bit by bit, in manageable chunks.

Why is it useful?
There is no complex terminology to get your head around, and you're only thinking about and working with one part of your body at a time, building up to a fully embodied physicality for your character.

How do I do it?
There follow four lists of prompts for you. It is fun to explore one section after the other, repeating several times over. For some, all this may offer too much detail, in which case choose one or two areas to concentrate on. The idea is to play with all these areas of physicality and see which ideas stick and feel helpful for your character.

1. Head, face and neck
Concentrate only on your head, face and neck.

- What might the audience notice about your face as you/your character come onto the stage?
- Think about how your character's face shows emotions/feelings.
- Does your character show their emotions clearly on their face or do they mask their feelings (have a 'poker face')?
- Does your character look others directly in the eye, or do they look away, down, or in another direction? Why? (This is a good indicator of your character's

confidence level, or else if they're lying or distracted.)
- Does your character have a signature facial expression, or 'resting face'? Do they tend to smile, sneer, grimace?
- Does this change throughout the play?
- Does the character have a physical impairment (blindness, deafness, missing teeth, stiff neck)? These will affect how the character moves his/her head and face.
- If the character is older than you, how do the head and neck present?
- If the character is younger than you, how do the head and neck differ to your own?

2. Upper body (shoulders, arms, hands, chest, stomach)
Now consider everything above your hips.

- Does the character have good posture? Do they stand up straight or slouch?
- Does the character swing their arms when they walk, or hold them tightly at their sides? Do they cross their arms, hug themselves, or wring their hands?
- How big are the character's gestures? Do they use their hands while they speak?
- Do they touch other characters? Which ones? How do they touch them?
- Does the character breathe deeply or take shallow breaths? Is breathing easy or difficult?

3. Lower body (lower back, hips, pelvis, legs, feet)
Move your attention down to your lower body.

- Does the character move slowly or quickly? Why? Do they bowl, limp or stumble?
- Is the character light on their feet or do they plod and stomp along? Do they lift their feet when they walk? Do the character's feet turn inwards or outwards when they walk? Do they walk heel-first or toe-first?

3. Leading parts

What is it?
Identifying the part of the body that your character leads from when they move.

Why is it useful?
It gives you one simple thing to focus on but can be really transformative. The choice of body part can be a clear marker of status and of character traits.

How do I do it?
Think about your character's personality traits. What is important to them? Is your character a drunk who is always thinking about what they can put in their belly? Is your character a snooty person who looks down on other people?

Experiment by walking around the space leading with different isolated body parts. For the drunken character, try leading with your gut, as if you have a rope tied around your waist and are being pulled forward by it.

Part Two: Your Skills

For the snooty character, what happens if you lead with your chin, or your nose?

Consider all areas, and try them out to see what you discover. Try with your forehead, your knees, your chest, your eyes, try with just one side of your body. Notice what all of these options do to your sense of your character's status.

While you're exploring you can really exaggerate this, but once you land on something that works it may be so subtle that only you know you're doing it.

4. Props

What is it?
Exploring whether interacting with certain objects helps you to feel connected to your character.

Why is it useful?
In the early stages of finding a character it can sometimes be difficult to know what to do with your hands, and you can become stiff or awkward because you are trying to embody someone else without anything to help you. A prop can work like a trigger to help you find the character's physicality.

How do I do it?
Instead of asking yourself 'how do I move as this character?' Try asking yourself 'how do I interact with this

object?' If you pick up a pen, does your character hold it tight, fiddle with it, chew the end?

Is there an object which makes your character feel safe, comfortable, important? A clip-board, a mobile phone, a handbag? How does your character hold their cup of tea? Are there any impulses that help you to access the physicality of your character because of the prop?

Ultimately you will not be holding any prop you find useful for an entire performance, but in the exploration stages it might help you to find out some things about the way your character moves.

5. Animal studies

What is it?
Choosing an animal which you feel represents the key character traits of your character, and observing its physicality to add to your toolkit in portraying the movement of that character.

Why is it useful?
There are a huge variety of ways in which human beings move. The animal kingdom offers a wide spectrum of movement styles and they can be easier to see than the subtle differences between humans. Applying animal characteristics to human characters gives you much greater freedom of expression.

How do I do it?

Think about your character's traits. Are they confident and bolshy, are they shy, or nervous? Are they nosy, exciteable, haughty, or thoughtful?

Now consider animals that you feel inhabit these characteristics. Find footage of your chosen animal, or even better, go to the zoo, and really observe the movements in front of you. Begin by imitating the animal's movements, playfully and freely. Notice if any aspect of that imitation is useful for the creation of your human character – the way they hold their head, the speed of their movement, and so on.

Don't settle on one animal straight away, explore and play and you might be surprised what you discover.

Text

There is no 'quick' fix to acting. Going slowly is empowering, and extracting detail is the job of the actor. In this section there are lots and lots of strategies for understanding text and lifting it off the page.

> **Goals and obstacles**
>
> **Goal**
> To analyse and understand the text well enough to bring it to life off the page.
>
> **Obstacles**
>
> - Dyslexic people don't like words and text
> - Knowing how to do it – where to start
> - Self-doubt about your process.

To overcome these obstacles we will work through a process with strategies for each of the following aspects:

- Research
- Understanding the text
- Navigating the play
- Getting to know your character
- Bringing the lines to life

You can work through in order, or you can jump to whichever bit you're ready to work on right now.

All strategies are just suggestions for you to consider. Nothing is right or wrong. And have fun!

Research

Research helps to build the world of the play. It offers the big picture. You should do your own research ahead of the first rehearsal of any play.

Why bother?
Research is a foundation from which to begin. It can be creatively inspiring and help you find the 'magic' in your work. The information you discover as you go along will sit quietly fermenting in your mind. If you take the layered, multi-sensory approach to your learning and capturing of information, it will gradually be absorbed through your different senses, building up inside you to create a foundation of knowledge.

Strategies

1. Discovering the plot – What is going on?!

What is it?
Here are some dyslexic friendly ways of processing what is happening in the play so that you understand the text clearly.

Why is it useful?
For a dyslexic person there is no point in being told to 'read the play three times' when you don't process what you read as you read it. Thinking outside the box and applying layered methods which appeal to different senses will help you process information.

How do I do it?
- Read an abridged (shortened) version of the play.
- Find a summary of the plot.

- Watch different versions of the play, live or filmed. (Seeing a selection of interpretations and versions opens your awareness and deepens your understanding, so do not limit it to one specific version. Always remember that your director will then need you to be flexible and open to seeing their interpretation of the work, and not the specifics of what you have watched).
- Download an education pack from a theatre/school/university, if one is available for the play: these offer concise chunks of information and keep it simple. Here is an example of an education pack from the Royal Shakespeare Company which offers an introduction to *Macbeth*: www.rsc.org.uk/macbeth/education
- Draw a mind-map or chart of the characters and how they relate to each other.
- Act out (mime) in a playful way what main events happen in each scene.
- Speak aloud the action of the play as though you're explaining it to a ten-year-old.
- Describe the play to another person in a simple informal summary of a few sentences.
- Map out the plot around a room, with different signs, labels or furniture to represent different locations, characters or families.
- Listen to directors' interviews and watch YouTube videos of actors discussing the plot of the play, from past productions.

Capture feelings, atmospheres and big picture thoughts about the story. Keep your findings with you in a folder, a scrapbook, a notepad, a box or an ideas-board.

2. Collect images related to the play

What is it?
Creating a visually stimulating world of the play to help you enter into it.

Why is it useful?
Creating something visual works for many dyslexic actors. It opens up the play's world, and forms a visual record, so you can refer back to it whenever you like and refresh your memory. It'll also serve as a reminder of all the work you've done as it builds and builds and builds. This will increase your confidence in rehearsal.

How do I do it?
Collect photos and images of people, places, objects, text, materials, and visual reminders of atmospheres, colours, smells, music – whatever connects to the play for you, as you research.

Stick them on a:
- Bedroom or study wall
- Scrap book
- Pinterest board
- Laptop
- Notebook
- Collage
- Mind-map.

3. Mine the playwright for clues

What is it?
Finding out as much info as possible about the author of the play.

Why is it useful?
Authors often project an aspect of their life into their work, and any similarities between the playwright and the plot or characters will help you understand the play.

How do I do it?
Ask yourself these questions:
- What other works has the author written?
- When were they writing?
- What were their life events?
- What propelled them to write the play?

Find answers:
- Online (for example on Wikipedia)
- In libraries.

4. The big picture of the play

What is it?
This exercise involves collecting general facts about the play and its context.

Why is it useful?
It gives you a greater and more detailed understanding of the world of the play.

How do I do it?
Go through the text and work out:

- How many acts are there?
- How many scenes are there?
- How many scenes are you in?
- What is the language style?
- What are the overall themes of the play?
- What time-period is it set in?
- When was it written, and why?
- What country does it take place in?
- What are the main events that happen in the play?
- What were the political events in the country and other countries around the world at that time?

5. Timeline of the play

What is it?
Drawing up a timeline to understand what is happening in the play and when it happens, using a roll of paper.

Why is it useful?
Seeing all the events laid out before you is a great way to understand the arc of the play and the timespan over which the play takes place. This can also be useful later in rehearsal when thinking about the given circumstances of each scene.

How do I do it?
Here is an example showing a timeline for Lady Macbeth. This strategy can be used to mark the key moments for a single character like this, or you can draw out a timeline of a whole play with detail for every scene, depending on your needs.

The Dyslexic Actor

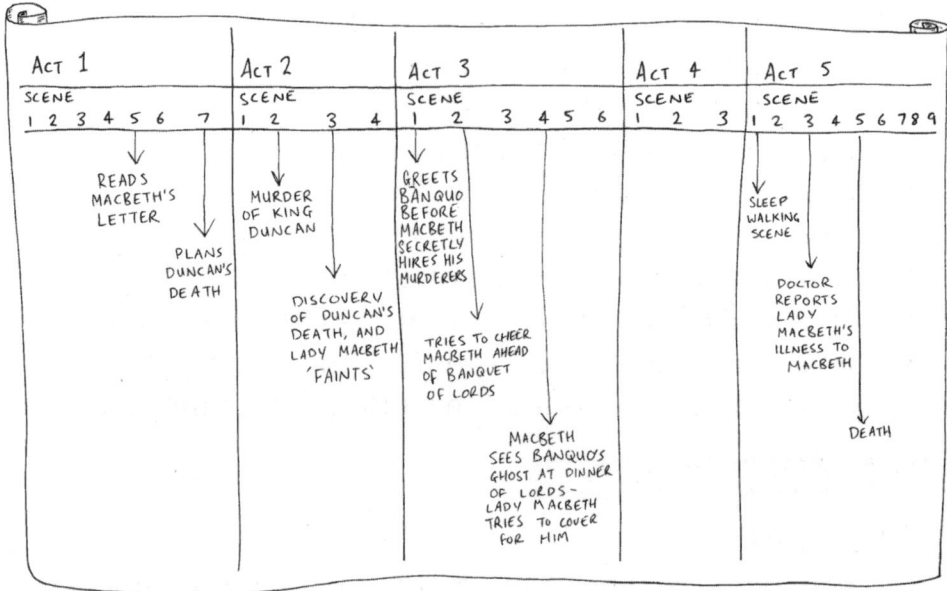

1. On a roll of paper mark the acts from left to right.
2. Add scenes below the acts.
3. Fill in the key events for your character in all the scenes they appear in.
4. If it helps you to visualise where you are in the play, add images to your timeline.

You can put this chart up on the wall in your rehearsal room or at home, and you can keep a small version in your script if that is useful.

It can be as detailed or as basic as suits your needs. You may like to begin with marking basic milestones and keeping that information simple for the first few days, after which time another layer of information can be added as you discover more.

6. People

What is it?
Finding out who all the characters in the play are.

Why is it useful?
A wider understanding of the characters in the play is essential to help you build your own character's relationships with other people.

How do I do it?
1. Write down the names of the characters in the play.
2. Now explore the relationships and hierarchical structure between the characters:

    - What relationships do the characters have with any other characters in the play?
    - Who holds the power?
    - Do the characters like each other?
    - What grievances do they hold against each other?

Capture what you discover in your scrapbook, with diagrams or lists or drawings.

7. Places

What is it?
Finding out where the places referenced in the script are, and what they're like.

Why is it useful?
This exercise helps your imagination. It grounds you in where you are and makes the world of the play come alive.

How do I do it?
Think about these questions and record your answers, checking in with all your senses to build an image – sight, hearing, touch, taste and smell:

- What country and city are you in?
- Where was the play originally set?
- Does it feel modern or historical?
- What does the geography and physical landscape look and feel like?
- What's the weather like?
- What's the architecture of buildings like?
- What's the culture of that place like?
- What's its music, art and literature like?

8. Aesthetics – look and feel

What is it?
Finding out about the aesthetics of the world in which the play is set.

Why is it useful?
This is another exercise which helps your imagination and grounds you in the world of the play.

How do I do it?
Think about what the clothes, fashions, uniforms, furniture, accessories, technology and gadgets in this world look like.

Find images and add them to a mood board: your mind may usefully hold on to these images to give you a wider imaginative sense of the play's setting.

9. Enter the world of the play

What is it?
This exercise is about immersing yourself in the world of the play.

Why is it useful?
Immersing yourself helps you understand the world of the play better, whilst also allowing you to be playful.

How do I do it?
Here is an example. If you are working on a traditionally set production of *Macbeth*, you might, for part of a day, decide to:

- Wear some clothing that evokes living in a Scottish castle in the eleventh century.
- Create a soundscape recording to listen to.
- Consider that candlelight and firelight were the only means of light and heat: turn the heating off and try to imagine having stone walls and no carpet.
- Research what food might have been eaten in Scotland at that time – is it something you can try?
- Find out what would be under your feet: mud, stone, straw? Can you re-create this and experience it?
- Do whatever else you feel curious to do, so as to explore this world you are reading about.

> **Remember!**
>
> These strategies are here for you to play with.
>
> Layered on top of each other they will definitely give you a deep understanding of the text you're working on.
>
> Individually, they are ways of exploring whether you absorb information more ably one way or another.
>
> Only in trying them all will you know. But once you know – the knowledge is with you for your whole career.

Understanding the text

You have a foundation of knowledge inside you from the work you've done on research. Now let's have a go at analysing what is written. Exploring the words, and analysing the text in detail, gives you 'evidence' as to who your character is and how you relate to other people. It also makes line-learning far easier, as learning is always best supported by understanding.

This section provides you with the foundational detective work that will lead you to discover your character and to embody the text you need to hear and speak. There is no pressure to remember anything at this stage, but you'll begin to find that you do. Go slowly, go methodically. This 'work' needs to be done. And this work takes time!

Why bother?
Exploring text analysis will open up so many more creative choices for you!

> Always remember to reflect on what you notice after each strategy.

Strategies

1. Prep your text

What is it?
Make a copy of your script and stick the pages on bigger paper so you can write your analysis and thoughts directly next to the bit of text that they apply to.

Why is it useful?
It puts all your thoughts and ideas about the text nice and clearly in one place.

How do I do it?
Stick each page of the photocopied script on to a larger piece of paper so you have room to write around it.

Use a ring binder and insert blank pages in between the pages for writings and drawings. You need plenty of spare paper for scribbling on.

You may need to make several copies of the script so that you can employ more than one of the strategies listed below.

2. Difficult words

What is it?
Finding out the meaning of all the words you don't know or understand.

Why is it useful?
When you are reading your script, don't skip over words that are a bit more tricky. If you've any doubt about the precise meaning of a word, be curious and look it up. It's very possible to discover that a word you thought you understood actually has a slightly different meaning. Knowing the precise meanings of words will infiltrate your acting and make the thoughts you have as a character and the way you deliver your lines more specific. Specific acting = better acting!

How do I do it?
1. Take a difficult word and look up its meaning.
2. Write the meaning of the word on the page.
3. Say the word and its meaning aloud.
4. Perhaps draw an image for this word.

3. Punctuation

What is it?
Mark all the punctuation in your text, for you to get the 'gist' of what's being said.

Why is it useful?
Punctuation makes sense of a text. It tells you where to breathe, and breaks up thoughts. Analysing the punctuation will help you understand exactly what it is your character is saying.

> Breathing is connected to thoughts. When we have a new thought, we breathe – taking in air in order to have breath to articulate it!

How do I do it?
1. Take a pencil, and draw a slash or a vertical line at the end of every sentence, where the full stops are.
2. These slashes show you when to breathe.
3. Now go through the text, speaking it aloud, and breathing at the end of every sentence.
4. Listen to yourself as you speak. Do you pick up more of a sense of what is being said? Be sure to understand everything you are saying.

Punctuation marks

Remember that colons (:) and semicolons (;) do not mark the end of sentences. They link parts of the same sentence together.

- A colon (:) is used to mean 'because' or 'therefore', or before expanding on an idea that has been introduced.
- A semicolon (;) means 'and'.

A 'thought' continues through colons (:) and semicolons (;) until the end of a sentence – until you reach a full stop (.), question mark (?), or an exclamation mark (!).

Here is an example:

> **From *Driftwood* by Tim Foley (Part One, page 5)**
>
> TINY. So the plan is to gather all the driftwood. / Make a pyre nearby. / We lay Dad atop of it, set him alight. / And the people on our road, from our church, they come on down, gather round, and we all just (*Inhales. Exhales. Inhales. Exhales.*)
>
> MARK. What's going on.
>
> TINY. We're breathing in Dad. / Cos he's smoke by this point isn't he. / Solid into liquid into gas, remember that from school. / Dad's the solid. / Dunno what the liquid is, maybe the sea, but the smoke is the gas. / Smoke with bits of Dad. / Microscopic, air particles, ash. / Sort of be like, comforting. / Like warm, all hot on your chest, wearing a scarf, having a lil whiskey. / I'll get someone on the music, there's a man with a guitar by the huts once a week, the huts are new. / The man's new too, but he's also pretty old. / And the songs are even older. / Pub closed down but we'll pick up some tinnies. / Kick-off at dusk. / Fire goes till dawn
>
> MARK (*beat*). We are not doing any of that
>
> TINY. I mean I'd have to get a permit

4. Mark the thoughts

What is it?
Going through the text you speak and clearly marking each different thought.

Why is it useful?
It is important to differentiate between thoughts so that each idea makes sense and feels new in the moment.

How do I do it?
Start by separating the questions from the statements. Highlight all the statements in one colour and underline all the questions in another. Then look at where each thought comes to an end and a new one begins. Put slashes in the text between each thought. Each of these thoughts are said differently from each other.

Here is an example:

> **From *Two Billion Beats* by Sonali Bhattacharyya (Scene 3, page 33)**
>
> ASHA. I mean, Mum's talking to me again, yeah? / Really talking to me. / Telling me stuff I've never known before. / So what am I supposed to do? / She told me about this friend she had, growing up. / Her best friend. Mariam. / How they totally bonded, right from reception, did everything together. / They had this pact to go to the same uni, get a flatshare, the works. / But then they grew apart in their last year in sixth form because Mariam started to have

weirder and weirder views. / Started playing up in class. / Finding trouble where there wasn't any. / Fell out with all the teachers, even Mrs Osbourne who did English Literature and Mum loved her. / She was reading all these books and pamphlets. Stuff she would've got into bare trouble for if anyone else knew. / Mum reckons if it happened now people would say she was being 'radicalised'. / Mum tried talking to her and Mariam tried to push her away. / But Mum says you don't leave it like that, not if you love someone.

5. Turning the text into your own words

What is it?
Turning each line into something you'd say in your own words and writing it out.

Why is it useful?
This 'translating' exercise makes sure you understand what you are hearing and saying. It is particularly useful for classical text, which can feel like another language. It is also useful if you are working with modern text that has been written in a different dialect to your own.

How do I do it?
Here is an example. *Imperium: The Cicero Plays* are set in ancient Rome and written in modern English, but the language is quite formal:

Part Two: Your Skills

From *Imperium: The Cicero Plays*, based on the Cicero trilogy by Robert Harris, adapted by Mike Poulton (*Caesar*, Scene 2)	A 'translation' by me
CICERO. For a man with no fear of death, Caesar – you certainly travel with a large bodyguard.	CICERO. You say you're not scared. Liar, look at the size of your bodyguard.
Laughter – CAESAR *remains unreadable.*	*People laugh* – CAESAR *doesn't react.*
CAESAR. As Head of State I have a responsibility to the People – to the nation. Rome needs me more than I need Rome.	CAESAR. I've got to look after the people of Rome, they really need me.
CICERO. And what of the soul? Do you believe the soul immortal? Or is it extinguished as the body dies?	CICERO. And what about the soul of a person? Does it die when a person is dead?
CAESAR. How can we know? What does it matter? In my own case the question is irrelevant. The soul of Caesar shall live in eternity. Naturally. Because I'm a god.	CAESAR. How do I know? It doesn't matter for me, I shall always live on because I'm a God.

Here is a second example. *Red Pitch* is set in a South London football ground, and the language is informal:

From *Red Pitch* by Tyrell Williams (Scene 9, page 56)	**A 'translation' by me**
JOEY. [...] I was speaking to the kit lady and I started deeping it – without you man, I wouldn't have got in. She was asking me how did I get so good, did I have special training... I was like na, I just played Sunday League and kicked ball with my boys. Who knows if I would've done the Sunday League thing if it weren't for you man. All them times you shouted me to come Red Pitch. Putting me in goal. You man trained me up.	JOEY. [...] I was talking to the lady who hands out the football kit and I started getting deep and meaningful. Without you I wouldn't have got in. She was asking me how did I get so good at football, did I have special training... I said no, I just played in the Sunday League and kicked a ball with my mates. Who knows if I would have joined the Sunday League if it weren't for you. All the times you got me to come to the Red Football Pitch. You made me play goalkeeper. You trained me.

Repeat this exercise for all of the scenes you're in. If you are struggling to 'translate' anything that is said, remember that context is key. Don't look at the line on its own, but think about how it fits into the context of the scene and the play – this should give you clues to understanding what the character is saying in that moment.

It is also just as important to write out your scene partner's lines in your own words, as you must understand what is being said to you, not only what you say!

6. The first words

What is it?
Highlighting the first word of every sentence with a coloured highlighter.

Why is it useful?
Especially in a large chunk of dense text, underlining the first word of each sentence may tell you something about what your character is saying and feeling. This can therefore help you to trace the emotional structure of the scene.

How do I do it?
1. Take the printed text and a highlighter.
2. Highlight the first word in every sentence.
3. Say just these words out loud.
4. What sense do you get of your character's journey through that speech/scene?

Here is an example:

The Dyslexic Actor

From *A Sudden Violent Burst of Rain* by Sami Ibrahim (page 11)

ELIF. […] It starts with butterflies in your stomach.
A single butterfly.
Big one: churning and flapping.
Feels good.
No: it feels terrifying.
Night and day.
And Elif could barely concentrate because of that fucking boy, with a smile she couldn't say no to.

One day she kissed him.
He kissed her back.
Then he took out a necklace – beautiful polished pearls – and placed it around her neck.
Elif felt their cool indent on her skin, she smiled at him.
And then she had to leave.
As she left, the butterfly flapped frantically.
She felt it endlessly.
As she worked.
As she travelled.
That butterfly would not stop flapping and so

She took a deep breath.
Calmed herself.
She reached down into her throat.
Right the way down.
Her fingers feeling their way through her body.
Into her tingling stomach.

Part Two: Your Skills

> **She** caught it.
> **This** butterfly.
> **She** lifted it out.
> **Held** it in her clasped hand.
> **Saw** its wings flapping.
> **Then** slowing.
> **Then** stopping.
> **The** wings detached and fell to the ground like autumn leaves.
> **The** body remained in her hand.
> **It** was a small seed.
> **She** didn't know what to do with it.
> **She** was stood near a river, she thought about throwing it in.
> **But** she couldn't bring herself to.
> **Instead**, Elif took the seed over to her cart and found a terracotta pot.
> **She** filled it with soil, and then, with her little finger, she hollowed out a small hole.
> **She** placed the butterfly's body inside and buried it.

What do you notice?

7. Famous last words

What is it?
Highlighting the last word of every sentence.

Why is it useful?
Highlighting the last word may also tell you something about what you are saying or how you feel. This strategy

is particularly useful for Shakespeare soliloquies – it can offer you a helpful map through the text.

How do I do it?
1. Take the printed text and a highlighter.
2. Highlight the last word in every sentence.
3. Say just these words out loud.
4. What sense do you get of your character's journey through that speech/scene?

Here is an example:

> **From *A Sudden Violent Burst of Rain* by Sami Ibrahim (page 11)**
>
> ELIF. [...] It starts with butterflies in your ==stomach==.
> A single ==butterfly==.
> Big one: churning and ==flapping==.
> Feels ==good==.
> No: it feels ==terrifying==.
> Night and ==day==.
> And Elif could barely concentrate because of that fucking boy, with a smile she couldn't say no ==to==.
>
> One day she kissed ==him==.
> He kissed her ==back==.
> Then he took out a necklace – beautiful polished pearls – and placed it around her ==neck==.
> Elif felt their cool indent on her skin, she smiled at ==him==.
> And then she had to ==leave==.

As she left, the butterfly flapped frantically.
She felt it endlessly.
As she worked.
As she travelled.
That butterfly would not stop flapping and so

She took a deep breath.
Calmed herself.
She reached down into her throat.
Right the way down.
Her fingers feeling their way through her body.
Into her tingling stomach.
She caught it.
This butterfly.
She lifted it out.
Held it in her clasped hand.
Saw its wings flapping.
Then slowing.
Then stopping.
The wings detached and fell to the ground like autumn leaves.
The body remained in her hand.
It was a small seed.
She didn't know what to do with it.
She was stood near a river, she thought about throwing it in.
But she couldn't bring herself to.
Instead, Elif took the seed over to her cart and found a terracotta pot.
She filled it with soil, and then, with her little finger,

> she hollowed out a small hole.
> She placed the butterfly's body inside and buried it.

What do you notice?

8. Verbs: finding the action

What is it?
Underlining the verbs in each sentence.

Why is it useful?
Verbs are actions – 'doing' words. These underlined words will tell you what action is happening in your text.

How do I do it?
1. Take a sentence from the text, and locate the verb in it, for example 'to go', 'seeing', 'swim', 'heard', or 'explore'. Every full sentence should have at least one verb. If you are unsure, ask yourself 'is this word a thing I can *do*?' e.g. 'I go', 'I see', 'I swim', 'I hear', I explore'.
2. Take a pencil or a coloured pen and underline the verb.
3. Repeat this for all sentences.
4. Now speak the verbs out loud and notice what action is taking place or being described.
5. If you are ever unsure of how to deliver a line, a helpful tip can be to focus on the verb. Read the line and put the stress on the verb. Suddenly you'll see the line make sense!

Here is an example:

From *A Sudden Violent Burst of Rain* by Sami Ibrahim (page 11)

ELIF. [...] It <u>starts</u> with butterflies in your stomach.
A single butterfly.
Big one: <u>churning</u> and <u>flapping</u>.
<u>Feels</u> good.
No: it <u>feels</u> terrifying.
Night and day.
And Elif could barely <u>concentrate</u> because of that fucking boy, with a smile she couldn't <u>say</u> no to.

One day she <u>kissed</u> him.
He <u>kissed</u> her back.
Then he <u>took</u> out a necklace – beautiful polished pearls – and <u>placed</u> it around her neck.
Elif <u>felt</u> their cool indent on her skin, she <u>smiled</u> at him.
And then she had to <u>leave</u>.
As she <u>left</u>, the butterfly <u>flapped</u> frantically.
She <u>felt</u> it endlessly.
As she <u>worked</u>.
As she <u>travelled</u>.
That butterfly would not <u>stop</u> <u>flapping</u> and so

She <u>took</u> a deep breath.
<u>Calmed</u> herself.
She <u>reached</u> down into her throat.
Right the way down.
Her fingers <u>feeling</u> their way through her body.
Into her tingling stomach.

She <u>caught</u> it.
This butterfly.
She <u>lifted</u> it out.
<u>Held</u> it in her clasped hand.
<u>Saw</u> its wings <u>flapping</u>.
Then <u>slowing</u>.
Then <u>stopping</u>.
The wings <u>detached</u> and <u>fell</u> to the ground like autumn leaves.
The body <u>remained</u> in her hand.
It <u>was</u> a small seed.
She didn't <u>know</u> what to <u>do</u> with it.
She was <u>stood</u> near a river, she <u>thought</u> about throwing it in.
But she couldn't <u>bring</u> herself to.
Instead, Elif <u>took</u> the seed over to her cart and <u>found</u> a terracotta pot.
She <u>filled</u> it with soil, and then, with her little finger, she <u>hollowed</u> out a small hole.
She <u>placed</u> the butterfly's body inside and <u>buried</u> it.

9. Nouns: building images

What is it?
Highlighting the nouns in each sentence.

Why is it useful?
A noun is a word for a person, place or thing. If you become familiar with these 'things' and they form images in your mind, the text will be easier both to understand and later to remember.

Part Two: Your Skills

How do I do it?

1. Take a highlighter, and highlight each noun in your text.
2. Be specific about the images you have in your mind's eye for each noun: e.g. if it's a house, have a specific house in mind – maybe your old house, or the house relevant to the circumstances of your text.
3. If it helps, draw an image next to each noun.

Don't worry about memorising these things – if you just notice them, they'll gradually absorb themselves automatically into your memory.

Here is an example:

> **From *Pennyroyal* by Lucy Roslyn (Daff Alone, page 38)**
>
> DAFF. Chris and Drew did all this work on Mum's garden while I was away.
>
> Like, you can tell it's going to look nice. And Drew does a lot of woodwork out of the garage. He follows Chris round like a massive shadow. And I mean, he's a *beast* but he always brings these little packed lunches, and he'll offer you coffee from his thermos even though the kitchen is, like – it's just inside. And he'll give you the

WOODWORK

GARAGE

THERMOS

nice cup. The *nice* cup. And he'll look at you like... you can feel him looking at you. And you can feel him wondering what on *earth* to do about it. He'll be peeping over the brim. He'll be looking at you like... (*To be wanted*, exhilarating.) I don't know how to describe it.

He's got a really nice *way* about him. He's a gentleman. In a monster body.

Remember! You may not want to do all of these strategies on one copy of your script as all the colour and underlining and other markings could become overwhelming. Make as many copies as you need to be able to do the strategies that are useful to you. Once you've got to know the text and your character really well, you might want to start rehearsals with a fresh copy altogether.

Navigating the play

Not all plays run chronologically, or forwards through time. Sometimes stories are told with flash-backs, or jumps in time. Sometimes several scenes in a play can take place in the same setting, or with the same combination of characters on stage, which can make it difficult to differentiate between them. Use some of the following strategies to help you clarify the journey of how the story unfolds.

Why bother?
Finding your way around the play is an important part of the preparation that will help you to stay on top of things once you get into rehearsals.

It will also play an important part in helping you to understand your character's emotional journey, allowing you to embody that character more truthfully.

Strategies

1. Titles

What is it?
Marking each scene with a name or image that captures that scene for you.

Why is it useful?
If you often get confused about what text is where in a play, giving each scene a name or a picture can help remind you what the different sections are, and allow you to quickly find your bearings.

How do I do it?
Go through each scene and come up with a name that summarises that scene for you.

Write the name you've chosen at the top of the scene.

If it's helpful for you, you can draw an image that summarises the scene – instead of, or next to, your new title.

Here is an example:

> **From *Macbeth* by William Shakespeare (Act 4, Scene 2)**
>
> Lady Macduff is married to Macduff, the Thane of Fife. Her appearance in the play is brief: she and her son are introduced in this climactic scene that ends with murder on Macbeth's orders. Macbeth has decided to kill Macduff's family after receiving the second set of prophecies from the witch.
>
> My Title – Murder of Lady Macduff and her Son

2. Putting your scenes in context

What is it?
Working out the emotional and physical context for each scene you are in.

Why is it useful?
You will understand better how your character feels, and

why they say and do the things they do in a scene, if you have worked out where they have come from and are going to.

How do I do it?
Ask yourself the following questions for each scene you are in. Sometimes the answers will be in the play, sometimes you might have to decide for yourself, or in collaboration with the director and other cast members.

Before this scene
- What has happened 24 hours before my scene?
- What has happened immediately before my scene?
- Where have I come from?

During this scene
- What year is it?
- Month?
- Season?
- Day?
- Weather?
- Where am I?
- City? Country?
- What kind of neighbourhood?
- What kind of building?
- What is the room like? What furniture and objects does it contain?
- Does my character feel comfortable?

After this scene
- Where do I go after my scene?
- Who will I be with when I get there?

3. What is my emotional journey through the play?

What is it?
Making a visual guide to the highs and lows of your character's journey through the story.

Why is it useful?
As well as giving you a clear picture of your emotional change through the whole play, this will help you to drop in to the correct emotional state when you are rehearsing scenes out of order.

How do I do it?
Draw a graph of your emotional journey.

1. Draw two axes – mark 'Emotional state' on the vertical axis and 'Timeline' on the horizontal axis.
2. Begin your timeline before the play, so that you can add the emotional context for your character before the story starts.
3. Add the acts and scenes to your timeline.
4. Draw a rough line which maps the highs and lows of your character's emotions as they run through the scenes.
5. Add colour in any way that you find useful.

You might find once you're in rehearsals that you need to re-draw this line as you discover things about your character.

When the director says 'We'll start with Scene 3', you can glance at your graph for a reminder of where your character is at emotionally, relative to the other scenes.

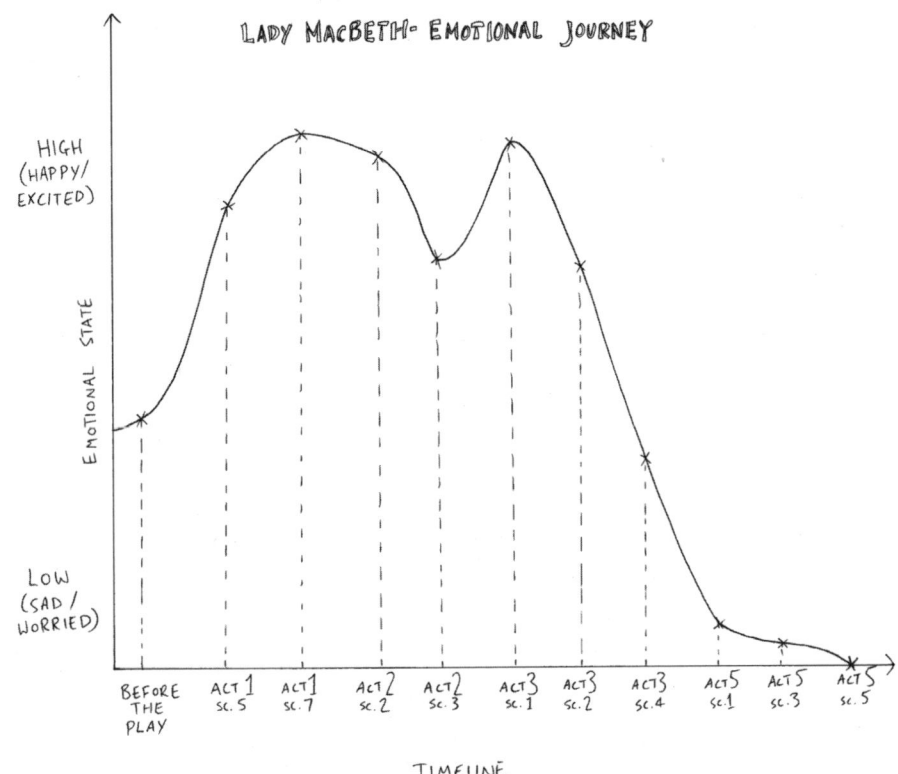

4. 'Chunking' the action – finding the beats

What is it?

This exercise marks any changes in the action/story of the play. Some directors will do this in rehearsals with all the actors together, so you are all aware of the moments in the story that need to be strongly communicated to the audience. They may call the resulting 'chunks' 'units', and will usually give those units a title, but you can use an image or symbol if you prefer. You can do it to a monologue as well as a whole scene.

Why is it useful?

Scenes can be long, but within them, there can be several significant moments of change, where, for example, a new character enters and changes the atmosphere, or some information is revealed which changes the feelings of the characters in the scene.

'Chunking' or 'uniting' the action marks these moments of change really clearly so that none get missed and the storytelling is clear. A 'unit' runs from one significant moment until the next.

How do I do it?

1. Go through your scenes from start to finish.
2. Mark a symbol for every entrance or exit of a character.
3. Mark a symbol or write a title for every time a character drops a bombshell. For example, in *Macbeth*, when the murderers admit that they failed to kill Banquo's son, you may write 'Fleance has escaped!'
4. Mark a symbol for anything else that seems useful to you. For example, if a character proposes to someone, draw a diamond ring.
5. You can draw a line right across your script each time you find one of these moments, so that one long scene might end up being divided into two, three, or even eight 'chunks' or 'units'.

Getting to know your character

Your character is something you should begin to discover ahead of rehearsals through your research into the play and analysis of the text.

In rehearsals your character will develop further, as you embody the words, thoughts and actions of the person you're playing.

Why bother?
The information you discover will gradually build as you proceed through the rehearsal process, and you will get to know your character in depth so that you can play it as truthfully as possible and with confidence.

Strategies

1. Facts about my character

What is it?
Mining the text for the facts about your character.

Why is it useful?
There is always going to be a strong element of imagination in your work as an actor, and you'll have to make things up to fill gaps in what the playwright has given you about the character, but it's good to start with what you can say you *know*.

How do I do it?
Go through the text and answer the following questions

about your character. Some answers will be in the text, others may not be. Begin only with the answers you can find in the text, then consider whether you need to research or decide upon the answers to the remaining questions.

- What's my full name?
- Does my name have a specific meaning?
- What's my nationality?
- What's my gender?
- What's my sexual history?
- What's my sexuality?
- Do I have an accent?
- What is my marital status and history?
- Who is my family?
- What is my health like?
- Am I wealthy?
- What is my profession and education?
- What is my social status and class?
- What are my religious beliefs?
- What are my hobbies?
- What are my eating and drinking habits?

2. Physical characteristics

What is it?
Mining the text for the facts about your character's physicality.

Why is it useful?
You have to embody the character physically as well as

emotionally, and find ways to do so even if they don't actually look or behave like you.

How do I do it?
See what you can find in the text to answer the following questions. If you can't find any evidence, consider what the answers might be and how those answers might need to affect your performance.

- How tall are you?
- How much do you weigh?
- What are your eyes like?
- What's your posture like?
- What are the mannerisms that make you unique?
- How do you move? Do you glide, stumble, dart, amble, roll?
- How happy are you with the above?
- How do you dress?
- Do you have tattoos, or scars?

3. My biography

What is it?
Writing your character's biography or CV.

Why is it useful?
This exercise will help you to pull together all the things you know or have decided about your character, but also give you an early opportunity to think as the character. If they were writing up their own CV or biography, what would they write?

The Dyslexic Actor

How do I do it?
Compile a biography of your character which pulls together all the facts you've gleaned from your mining of the text of the play.

Here is an example:

> Young Hamlet, Prince of Denmark, was born in the Castle of Elsinore to his father Old Hamlet and his mother Gertrude, King and Queen of Denmark. He was an only child and grew up with other members of his generation at the Danish court, including the daughter of his father's courtier, Ophelia, with whom he played in the castle gardens as a boy. Hamlet had a close relationship with his mother and looked up to his father as a great warrior and King. The Danish court was a God-fearing Christian environment. He went away to university in Gutenberg, Germany, at the age of fifteen, and enjoyed studying philosophy and the arts, and making a close-knit group of friends including other Danish ex-patriots. He particularly enjoyed taking part in and watching theatre, and was not a natural swordsman, despite fencing being a popular pastime among his peers.

4. Inside you

What is it?
Mining the text for information about your character's inner life, and filling in the gaps from your imagination.

Why is it useful?
It transports you inside the head of the character so that you can better imagine what it is like to be them.

How do I do it?
Search the play for answers to all or some of the following questions about your character. The answers to these questions are less likely to be in the text directly, you will have to deduce them – be a detective – or use your imagination. Be aware that as you rehearse you may find the answers to some of these questions changing – that's fine! This character will evolve with you.

- What is your personality like?
- What energy/atmosphere do you give off when dealing with others?
- What are your morals and ethics?
- Who do you like to mix and spend time with?
- What are your obsessions?
- How do you feel about yourself?
- Do you have any secrets?
- How do you feel about the world?
- What do you like about yourself?
- What would you change about yourself?
- What did you dream of being when you were a child? Are you this now?
- If you could have one thing, what would it be? What is stopping this?
- How happy are you with your life?
- What newspaper do you read? (What are your politics?)

- What is your greatest strength or gift?
- What has caused you to have any bad qualities?
- What do you wish for?
- What do you regret?
- What do you deny, or hide?
- What animal are you like?
- What is your most precious photo of?
- What is your guilty pleasure?
- Metaphorically, do you leave heavy prints on the floor, or light ones?

5. Jelly person character identity

What is it?
Taking the information you have gathered in the strategies above and filling it into a jelly person that represents your character.

Why is it useful?
It allows you to crystallise what you feel the important stuff is that goes together to make your character, and it serves as a physical reminder of that information.

How do I do it?
Draw an outline of a jelly person. Add inside the jelly person all the answers that were most useful to you from the questions you explored above. They should start with 'I am...', for example, 'I am a Prince.'

You will probably have to be selective unless your jelly person is huge, but this will force you to think about what is most important. You can add the physical characteristics to the outside of the jelly person and draw any props you feel might be relevant to your character e.g. walking stick, crown, etc.

This is your character. Stick it up on a wall somewhere so that you can revisit it if ever you're unsure how they might behave or feel.

6. How you see others

What is it?
Making a list of every sentence in the play where you say something about another person.

Why is it useful?
This exercise explores how you see other people, which gives you clues about what your character is like.

How do I do it?
Go through all your lines, starting from the beginning of the play.

Every time you say something about someone else, write it down.

Here is an example:

> **From *Pennyroyal* by Lucy Roslyn**
>
> In the following lines, the character Daff is describing someone she knows called Drew:
>
> 'Drew does a lot of woodwork out of the garage.'

> 'He's a *beast* but he always brings these little packed lunches.'
>
> 'He'll offer you coffee from his thermos.'
>
> 'He'll give you the nice cup.'
>
> 'He's got a really nice *way* about him.'
>
> 'He's a gentleman. In a monster body.'
>
> 'I have this friend who bragged that… she still wears the clothes of her youth, because she has the body of a teenager. And I thought… 'Great, well done! But *eugh*, fuck you.'
>
> We can deduce things about Daff from the positive way she speaks about Drew and also from her more negative thoughts about the other friend.

7. How others see you

What is it?
A list of every sentence in the play where someone says something about your character.

Why is it useful?
This exercise gives you clues about how other people view your character and interpret your character's behaviour. Sometimes, the things other people say about you are more honest than things you might say about yourself, so this strategy is a very important thing to do in combination with Strategy 6, in order to build a complete picture.

How do I do it?
Go through the whole play reading everyone else's lines.

Every time someone says something about your character, write it down.

Here is an example:

> **From *Imperium*: *The Cicero Plays*, based on the Cicero trilogy by Robert Harris, adapted by Mike Poulton (*Caesar*, Scene 2)**
>
> Imagine that you are playing Caesar.
>
> In the following lines, Cicero is talking to and about Caesar.
>
> CICERO. For a man with no fear of death, Caesar – you certainly travel with a large bodyguard.
>
> CICERO. We sit contemplating the 'if onlys' of history while Caesar and his gang dismantle our Republic.
>
> From these lines we can deduce some things about Caesar's character and behaviour.

8. What are my relationships to the other characters in the play?

What is it?
A list of the other characters in the play as they relate specifically to yours.

Why is it useful?
This exercise is another way to help you see how your character fits in to the wider community of the play.

How do I do it?
1. List your relationships with the other characters. Start with the simple facts, e.g. 'my mother', 'my husband's doctor'.
2. Now answer some less straightforward questions for yourself, where you may need to decide things not directly stated in the text:
   - Who is your best friend?
   - Who do you dislike the most? Why?
   - Are you in love with anyone?
   - Is anyone in love with you?
   - Is there a hierarchy of power to any of your relationships?

9. What do I want? (Objectives)

What is it?
A key part of the way that Stanislavsky encouraged actors to explore their character, this is about deciding what you feel your character wants in the play.

Why is it useful?
It's an incredibly effective way of helping you to understand what is driving all the actions and decisions your character makes in the play, and why they say everything they say. This in turn helps you to embody the character more truthfully, and to remember your lines.

Dyslexic actors often struggle with objectives and finding the courage to choose one. However, an objective is simply your reason for speaking. It is vital that you embody this objective so your performance is interesting to watch. Without it you're just reciting text!

How do I do it?
Now that you've read through the text and got to know your character really closely, think about what your character is trying to get from people.

Examine what you say and do. For example, if in the scene you're having an argument and your partner walks away in a huff, but then you try and make them stay, it means your objective is more than just to hurt them. It might be something like 'I want you to listen', or 'I want you to hear me out', or 'I want you to stay'.

- What is the one thing I really want throughout the whole play?
- Why do I need to have this so badly?
- What tactics can I use to get what I want? (e.g. deceiving people, charming people, etc…)
- What smaller things do I want, scene by scene? Give each scene an objective: 'in this scene I want…'

After exploring some or all of these exercises, you will have noticed what seems to work for you and what doesn't work so well. Remember this for next time. You are well on the way to rehearsal!

Bringing the lines to life

Bringing the text to life is about lifting it off the page and making the words of the playwright feel (to you and the audience) like they are your own – 'you', the character.

Why bother?

For dyslexic actors more than anyone, reading script aloud can be difficult, and learning and remembering lines can be difficult. This can mean that it is harder to connect to the thoughts and feelings behind the words – as you are tied up in the fact of what the words *are*. These strategies are designed to help you free yourself from those challenges, so that you can focus on being truthful in the role you are playing.

Strategies

1. Near and far distance

What is it?
The idea of this exercise is to experiment with different distances between you and the person you are speaking to.

Why is it useful?
You always act in a space. The space/distance between you and the person you are reacting to is active and dynamic. Different distances evoke different feelings. 'Are you okay?' called from one person to another at opposite ends of a garden, and 'are you okay?' spoken sitting next to a person,

suggest different things to an audience. This exercise is playful and has no specific outcome, but it will allow you explore the different possibilities of the space and different kinds of line delivery, and their emotional impact.

How do I do it?
- Stand in the centre of the space.
- Speak your first line from the centre to the person you are talking or reacting to.
- Experiment with moving closer to them as you say the line.
- Experiment with moving further away.
- What do your senses tell you? What are your sensations from this?
- Try again, using different volumes – from a whisper to speaking loudly, both close and far away.
- Try with other lines – which lines pull you towards the other character, and which pull you away?
- Do you want to be heard by the other person?
- Are they listening to you?
- How are your words affecting them?
- Are you achieving your objective? How does this change at different distances and volumes?

There's no right way – just play.

2. Ghost prompt

What is it?
Getting a friend or a recording to feed you the lines one by one, so you can concentrate on thought and delivery.

Why is it useful?
This exercise allows you to completely free your mind from trying to read or remember, so that you can just focus on playing with thoughts and delivery.

How do I do it?
- Ask a friend to act as the ghost at your side or behind you
- Get them to whisper a line of your text in your ear
- Repeat it after them
- How does this alter your line delivery?
- How does the thought before you speak alter how you say the line?

3. Supporting your objective with music

What is it?
Using music to inspire and support you in achieving your character's objective.

Why is it useful?
When we play music it affects our emotional state but also it affects us physically, because we naturally move and speak in the rhythm or mood of the music we are hearing.

If you are struggling to play the objective you have chosen, music can help you to access an emotional state that will support what you are trying to achieve.

How do I do it?
If a sportsperson were gearing themselves up for a big final race or tournament, they might put on music that makes them feel pumped up and powerful.

The emotional impact of music can be used as part of your preparation, to help you to embody the objective you have going into a scene.

For example, if your objective is 'I want to show you that I'm not afraid of you', then you might want to try running the scene with the song 'The Eye of the Tiger' playing.

If your objective is 'I want to soothe and comfort you', you might want to try running the scene with a gentle piece of classical music playing.

You can also try working against your objective. Find some music that reminds you of how you will feel if you *don't* get what you want. You can listen to this music before playing out the scene, or while the scene is running so that you have to push against the energy or emotions it brings up. This can bring some really interesting discoveries.

4. Get out of your head!

What is it?
Doing a task while you speak, to distract yourself from trying to 'do' things with the lines.

Why is it useful?
Actors, especially dyslexic actors, are constantly told to 'get out of their heads'. Perhaps you are thinking so hard about the lines that there is a block or disconnection between mind and body; the text is floating around in your mind and isn't a part of you in your body. It does not appear as though you are thinking the thoughts and

speaking the words for the first time, and so the scene loses its believability. This exercise helps you overcome this.

How do I do it?
Choose an activity (emptying the bin bag, unpacking the shopping) whilst delivering your text.

or

Build a pile of books and take one at a time to the other side of the room to make a new pile whilst delivering your text.

or

Throw sheets of paper around the room and run around collecting them up whilst delivering your text.

or

Take a pile of brightly coloured clothes and dot them around the room.

Begin your text whilst moving from t-shirt to jumper, jeans to coat, putting them on as you speak.

The idea is to make your focus 'the task' and not think about lines.

What do you notice when your focus is away from the text?

5. I'm not dull

What is it?
This exercise is about exploring and playing with variation in vocal pitch to stop dull line readings.

Why is it useful?
One of the strengths of the dyslexic ear can be hearing and easily absorbing rhythms and the musicality of speech. This is great for singing, but not always helpful for text. You don't want your gift for absorbing rhythms to lead to fixed and unrealistic line readings (the way in which an actor chooses to say lines). If you're not careful this can become the same time after time. Stale, and all on one level or tone. This exercise helps you break that.

How do I do it?
Move up and down in pitch as you are speaking the lines. Try it high pitch. Now try it low pitch.

There is no right way, so play about with your impulses. What do you notice? How does it affect you?

Try differing speeds. S-l-o-w and *faster*. Does this process open an option for a different delivery?

Add an accent that you love doing.

None of these versions are necessarily ways that you will say the line in performance but trying them out will help you to keep the line fresh, and you may make some discoveries.

6. Stomp it  L

What is it?
Actors speak in thoughts – not in sentences. Walking the thoughts as you say them is a way for your brain and body to acknowledge when the thought stops and changes to a new one.

Why is it useful?
Walking the thoughts clearly allows you to stop generalised acting.

How do I do it?
If you like to work in colours, take two different coloured pieces of paper or two different coloured articles of clothing.

Place them on the floor on each side of the room.

Stand by one colour, speak the thought aloud and walk to the other colour, to the full stop or change of thought. At this point you can stamp your foot to acknowledge the end of the thought/sentence, before you turn around to go back.

Turn around, breathe in, speak the new sentence (the new thought), and walk slowly to the other coloured garment and stamp your foot to acknowledge the end of that thought/sentence. Stomp.

This can be done to different pieces of furniture, clothes, coloured paper, etc. spaced all around the room. The important thing to remember is to move your body as you speak, stamping to acknowledge the end of the thought followed by physically turning.

Here is an example:

> **From the Prologue to *Henry V***
>
> Walk and speak out loud slowly, the first thought, in one direction:
>
> *O for a muse of fire, that would ascend the brightest heaven of* **invention**.
>
> Send the thought forward, with intention, to the last word of the line, and stomp. The last word of the line needs weight.
>
> Turn to the other colour.
>
> Take the next thought, the next sentence and move:
>
> *A kingdom for a stage, princes to act, and monarchs to behold the swelling* **scene**.
>
> Stomp.
>
> Continue doing this through the text.

Play around with the delivery of each thought. A new thought, more often than not, is said in a different way from the thought before. It is very easy to produce a glossed over delivery of generalised happiness or sadness; chanting in one dull tone of voice – this becomes uninteresting. A new thought must have the possibility to alter in speed and tone. It can be different every time.

Have fun exploring different possibilities. This is enough – to notice, acknowledge and to play. Don't over-think and feel uneasy at the thought of doing it right or wrong. Play.

Shakespeare

William Shakespeare represents the pinnacle of the English-speaking world's contribution to literature. His scripts are translated into more languages than any other works. This chapter explores how you can find working with Shakespearean text fulfilling, rich and meaningful. It also takes you through the necessary steps to help you act a monologue or role.

Why do many people avoid Shakespeare?

- It's dense and wordy
- All those strange and unknown words
- It's rarely performed well
- The 'rules' are complicated
- It feels like it's just for academics and 'posh' people
- 'It's boooooooring!'

- 'Pronouncing it is impossible!'
- 'I've got no idea what they're talking about!!'
- 'I don't know where to begin...'

And then try throwing in being dyslexic on top of all this!

But herein lies 'the rub'...! Shakespeare is fun.

He shows a unique insight into world experiences, and his plays exhibit a raw humanity that, as a dyslexic, you will relate to on many levels. Shakespeare's works are as relevant now as when he first wrote them more than four hundred years ago – a pretty amazing achievement! His stories are easily relatable: action-packed plots of wonderfully heightened drama full of murder, deceit, betrayal, love, family tradition, blood, guts and gruesomeness. It's all there to entice and enchant you, so don't be afraid. As you unravel his language, mythology, Italian comedy, Elizabethan culture, religion, war, marriage, English, Scottish and French history will start to unfold.

Why might Shakespeare be rewarding for you, the dyslexic actor?

The first thing to say is that if you can take on Shakespeare you can take on any text. The process and attention needed to do justice to his work will give you an education for life. Shakespeare was an ordinary person, like you. Shakespeare was also extraordinary, like you.

There are some interesting possible links between you and Shakespeare:

- Shakespeare was an actor himself
- Shakespeare loved playing. He enjoyed magic, monsters, mistaken identities
- Shakespeare probably left school at thirteen
- Shakespeare understood the human condition. He empathised with the marginalised
- Shakespeare knew what it was like to be under pressure to keep writing and hitting deadlines
- Shakespeare was a rule maker, and a rule breaker!

Do you notice anything in common?

Why can dyslexics be particularly good at Shakespeare?

Shakespeare thinks in pictures, images and colours. We know this from his text. He explains things by comparing them to other things – a rich language of metaphors and similes.

Shakespeare is perfect for the inquisitive, imaginative, courageous, curious and empathetic actor.

The rhythmic, musical nature of Shakespeare's work can help you learn the text.

Working out what Shakespeare is saying demands a process that, in turn, helps you to absorb and learn lines. There are no short-cuts. You might be used to finding short cuts in order to learn... Shakespeare won't let you: this process demands more of you.

Therefore, your self-esteem will grow. The way he used language enables expressivity, range and the possibility for you to excel. Playing a Shakespearean character will make you feel you've accomplished something really amazing.

Goals and obstacles

Goal
To be able to decipher and deliver Shakespeare's text with confidence, and to inhabit his characters truthfully.

Obstacles
- Unfamiliar language
- Negative preconceptions
- Lack of confidence.

Strategies

The strategies in this section are not so mix-and-match as other strategies in this book. It's more of a three-point plan to understanding Shakespearean text. We will look in order at:

1. Structure
2. Language
3. Character

1. Structure

Prose and verse

Distinguishing between prose and verse can be difficult for dyslexic actors, however, if you buy a good copy of the text you're working on, you will usually see a difference between prose and verse in terms of how it looks on the page. Prose looks like the text of a novel – it's in sentences and paragraphs, running right across the page. Verse looks like poetry – it's in lines, down the page.

Look at these two examples:

> **Example 1 – from *Macbeth***
>
> PORTER
> Here's a knocking indeed! If a man were porter of hell-gate, he should have old turning the key. [*Knocking within.*] Knock, knock, knock! Who's there, i' the name of Beelzebub? Here's a farmer that hanged himself on the expectation of plenty: come in time; have napkins enough about you; here you'll sweat for't. [*Knocking within.*] Knock, knock! Who's there, i' the other devil's name? Faith, here's an equivocator, that could swear in both the scales against either scale; who committed treason enough for God's sake, yet could not equivocate to heaven: O, come in, equivocator.

This is **prose**.

The word 'prose' comes from a Latin word meaning 'direct', and the phrase 'prosa oratio' meaning 'straightforward speech'. It refers to a mode of speaking or writing that doesn't contain the rhythmic rules or flowery ornaments of verse. Most modern plays are written in prose. It has no fixed rhythm to it and it has the feel of every-day speech.

> **Example 2 – from *Romeo and Juliet***
>
> BENVOLIO
> Madam, an hour before the worshipp'd sun
> Peer'd forth the golden window of the east,
> A troubled mind drave me to walk abroad;
> Where, underneath the grove of sycamore
> That westward rooteth from the city's side,
> So early walking did I see your son:
> Towards him I made, but he was ware of me
> And stole into the covert of the wood:
> I, measuring his affections by my own,
> Which then most sought where most might not be found,
> Being one too many by my weary self,
> Pursu'd my humour not pursuing his,
> And gladly shunn'd who gladly fled from me.

This is **verse**.

Verse is much more structured: it follows rules about the number of syllables in a line and which and how many of those syllables are stressed. Shakespeare's verse is written in iambic pentameter, which is explained in more detail below. As a general rule, if each line down the page begins with a capital letter, you are looking at verse.

In Shakespeare's texts, verse is used much more than prose, however, in keeping with the 'straightforward v. flowery' nature of the two, there is a noticeable divide along class lines. Upper class, educated characters speak mostly in formal verse, while lower class, less well-educated characters (who are also often the comic characters) speak in prose.

Iambic pentameter

What is it?
Iambic pentameter is a *metre* (a pattern of beats) made up of five (*penta*) *iambs*.

An *iamb* is a pair of beats: an unstressed beat followed by a stressed beat. 'Te-**dum**'

So in a line of iambic pentameter there are five of these 'iambs' – that adds up to ten syllables in total:

'Te-**dum**, te-**dum**, te-**dum**, te-**dum**, te-**dum**.'

Have a go now at beating this rhythm out with your hand.

This is the basic rhythm of each line of Shakespeare's verse.

How do I use it?
Early on when going over your text, you should mark the

beat of the iambic pentameter. This means marking the pulse or rhythm that Shakespeare intended the words to have.

1. Take a line of your text.
   e.g. *There is a willow grows aslant a brook*

2. Say it out loud slowly and count the number of syllables.

       1   2 3 4 5   6   7   8 9 10

   e.g. *There is a willow grows aslant a brook*

3. Now go through and draw a line under each second syllable (the stressed syllable).
   e.g. *There **is** a **wil**low **grows** as**lant** a **brook***

4. Now read the line out loud to yourself again, hearing the stresses in your voice as you read. Speak in rhythm while tapping it out with your hand or foot.

5. Repeat with all your lines of text.

The stress can help you work out the important words in the line. It is good to observe it, as it may help you to understand what you are saying. Sometimes it gives ideas about how to read the line or interpret it.

However, stresses are to be observed and explored in the early stages of analysing. It doesn't mean you should become trapped into a way of speaking, or that the delivery should be sing-songy. At this stage you are just noticing and feeling the rhythm of the words.

Word-shortening

Sometimes words with more syllables might be clipped (shortened) to make words fit the metre.

There are two examples of this in the speech by Benvolio from *Romeo and Juliet*, above:

'**Towards** him I made, but he was ware of me'

and

'I, **measuring** his affections by my own,'

The iambic pentameter requires that 'Towards' is treated as a one-syllable word, pronounced 'twards'. Meanwhile, 'measuring', which really has three syllables, becomes a two-syllable word in the line of iambic pentameter: 'mezring'.

Sometimes you can see this in the text, where an apostrophe is added to take out a syllable in a word. This also happens in the Benvolio speech, for example 'Peer'd' is just the word 'peered', but it is written with an apostrophe to show that it should be one syllable, not two as it would have been pronounced in Shakespeare's own time (peer-ed).

Shakespeare did some wrangling to achieve his iambic pentameter: some words switch from one syllable to two in the same sentence!

Just have a play, remembering to alternate stressed and unstressed syllables, and see what works.

Too many syllables!
Occasionally you will find a line with nine, eleven, twelve or even thirteen syllables. Shakespeare did not stick doggedly to the rules of verse – he played around with it, and used variation to help express the emotions of the characters.

If a character's speech has a lot of these extra syllables, or a lot of lines with syllables missing, it is worth asking yourself why they are not speaking in calm, measured, regular verse. Are they in a stressful situation? Are their emotions running high?

One of the best examples of this is Shakespeare's most famous speech of all: Hamlet's 'To be, or not to be'. In this speech he is contemplating suicide, and the emotional turmoil is reflected in the irregular line-lengths of his verse:

HAMLET
To be, or not to be: that is the ques**tion**:

                               One extra syllable at the end

Whether 'tis nobler in the mind to suf**fer**

                               One extra syllable at the end

> The slings and arrows of outrageous for**tune**,
>
>   One extra syllable at the end
>
> Or to take arms against a sea of trou**bles**,
>
>   One extra syllable at the end
>
> And by opposing, end them? **To** die: to sleep...
>
>   One extra unstressed syllable in the middle
>
> **Swapped stresses**
> If it absolutely only makes sense to stress the first beat of the line and not the usual second, this is ok – it even has a name: instead of an 'iamb', this '**Dum-**te' pattern is called a 'trochee'.
>
> There is a trochee in the second line of Hamlet's speech, above: '**Whe**ther'.

Shared lines

Shared lines are when two characters share a line of iambic pentameter between them. This really forces the actors to pick up their cues, so that they don't break the rhythm – and so the dialogue becomes really quick and snappy.

Here is an example from *Macbeth*:

LADY MACBETH
I heard the owl scream and the crickets cry.
Did not you speak?

MACBETH
                        When?

LADY MACBETH
                        Now.

MACBETH
                        As I descended?

The Dyslexic Actor

From *'Did not you speak?'* all the way to *'descended'*, is one line of iambic pentameter (with an extra syllable). This shows us the intensity of the situation and the heightened emotional states of the characters – which makes sense; Macbeth has just killed Duncan!

When performing shared lines, you need to bounce the energy between you like a ball. Keep it up in the air!

Sonnet

A sonnet is a poem with fourteen lines, written in iambic pentameter, and has a particular rhyme scheme. Shakespeare's sonnets always end with a rhyming couplet.

Shakespeare wrote 154 individual sonnets, some of which have become very famous, but he also wrote sonnets into three of his plays: *Romeo and Juliet*, *Henry V*, and *Love's Labour's Lost*.

When they first meet, Romeo and Juliet share a sonnet between them. This highlights the romantic idealism in their love at first sight:

> ROMEO
> If I profane with my unworthiest hand   1
> This holy shrine, the gentle fine is this: 2
> My lips, two blushing pilgrims, ready stand   3
> To smooth that rough touch with a tender kiss.   4
>
> JULIET
> Good pilgrim, you do wrong your hand too much,   5
> Which mannerly devotion shows in this;   6
> For saints have hands that pilgrims' hands do touch, 7

And palm to palm is holy palmers' kiss.	8
ROMEO	
Have not saints lips, and holy palmers too?	9
JULIET	
Ay, pilgrim, lips that they must use in prayer.	10
ROMEO	
O, then, dear saint, let lips do what hands do;	11
They pray, grant thou, lest faith turn to despair.	12
JULIET	
Saints do not move, though grant for prayers' sake.	13
ROMEO	
Then move not, while my prayer's effect I take.	14

2. Language

Shakespeare, Marlowe and their contemporaries wrote in a style that was very typical of the time. Symbols, imagination and emotions made up the basic recipe of performance. What a useful consideration for you as an actor, whose strengths are visual, imaginative and emotional intelligence.

Shakespeare, like all poets right up to the present day, used linguistic devices to create images and effects.

In a musical score there are indicators outlined for the singer or instrumentalist to help with speed, volume, stress and pitch. Language devices work a bit like this.

Although they work more like guidelines than rules to be followed, they allow you another useful route to explore, from which to develop an interpretation.

Here's a list with explanations of some of the most common language devices found in Shakespeare's work. They are grouped into categories: 'Sound', 'Structure' and 'Imagery'. Go through your text and make a note of them when they come up. They are hidden everywhere.

These devices are for you to 'notice' to bring depth and more understanding to your dialogue. They are not for you to learn or remember.

The following are enough to get you started!

Sound

Vowels

Vowel sounds (*a, e, i, o, u*) are often open sounds of emotion.

In the following example from *Much Ado About Nothing*, Beatrice cries out:

> BEATRICE
> **'O G_o_**d, that I were a m_a_n!
> I would **ea**t his h**ea**rt in the m_a_rketplace.'
>
> 'O's in Shakespeare are open vowel cries or sighs that come out of pure emotion.

Consonants

Consonants stop sound. They curb the openness of vowel sounds and have a more explosive feel in the mouth. They too can carry emotion, such as frustration in this example from *King Lear*:

> EDMUND
> Why **b**rand they us
> With '**b**ase,' with '**b**aseness,' '**b**astardy,' '**b**ase,' '**b**ase'–

Through his explosive 'b's we get a sense of Edmund's fury at the social constructs which look down upon illegitimate children like him, and bolster the fortune of legitimate children like his brother.

Alliteration

A series of words featuring the same, repeated consonant sound. This sound does not have to begin the word, it can be within it, however in the opening to this famous speech by Macbeth, it is the first letter of the words which stand out, emphasising the plodding inevitability of time passing:

> MACBETH
> **T**omorrow and **t**omorrow and **t**omorrow
> Creeps in this **p**etty **p**ace from **d**ay to **d**ay

Assonance

Alliteration for vowels, this is when the same sounding vowel occurs in words that are close to each other. It is sometimes called 'half rhyme'.

In the following example from *Hamlet*, you'll notice alliteration as well as assonance of 'eee' sounds:

> HAMLET
> Sp**ea**k the sp**ee**ch, I pray you, as I pronounc'd it to you, trippingly on the tongue.

It is fitting that Hamlet, who is instructing the players, should be demonstrating effective language techniques while he does so.

Structure

Antithesis

Antithesis is a contrast or opposition between two things, for example in Richard III when Anne says:

> ANNE
> For thou hast made **_the happy Earth_** thy **_hell_**

Caesura

A caesura is a natural break in the middle of a line of verse. The word 'caesura' comes from the Latin word for 'cut' as it is as if the line has been cut in half. Often, in more modern editions, the caesura will be visible by an item of punctuation such as a comma.

For example, in *The Winter's Tale*:

> ANTIGONUS
> It is for you we speak, not for ourselves.

And in *Hamlet*:

> **HAMLET**
> To be or not to be, that is the question.

You can see how in both of these lines there is a natural break which forces you to pause slightly.

Enjambment

It's important to remember that a *line* of Shakespearean verse is not the same as a *sentence*. Sometimes, a sentence runs on over several lines before reaching a full stop. This is called enjambment – it can have the effect of speeding up the lines because it pulls you on to read or speak the next one.

For example, when Juliet is waiting for nightfall and the return of Romeo, she says:

> **JULIET**
> And he will make the face of heaven so fine
> That all the world will be in love with night
> And pay no worship to the garish sun.

Lists

Shakespeare loves a list!

For example, in *Julius Caesar*, Portia says:

> **PORTIA**
> It will not let you eat, nor talk, nor sleep.

Remember, each word means a different thing, and you haven't thought of the word that is coming next – it just comes to you as you are speaking! Lists must be realistic, and the inflection in your voice will make them so or not.

Rule of three

The rule of three is when three things are listed for rhetorical effect. There is a rhythm to be found with three things that means they land more effectively with the listener: two items sounds unfinished and four sounds like too many. The reader or audience of this form of text is more likely to remember three things.

For example, in *Julius Caesar*, Mark Antony is a very powerful speaker, and begins his great persuasive speech using the rule of three:

> MARK ANTONY
> **Friends, Romans, countrymen**, lend me your ears

Imagery

For a dyslexic actor, lines can be absorbed far more easily if you picture the images created by Shakespeare's imagery:

Metaphor

A metaphor describes something by calling it something else.

For example:

> ROMEO
> It is the east, and **Juliet is the sun**

Romeo is calling Juliet the sun, thus telling us that like the sun Juliet is bright, warming everything she gazes on.

Simile
A simile compares something with something else.

For example, in *Othello*, Iago says he suspects Othello of sleeping with his wife:

> IAGO
> ...The thought whereof
> Doth, **like a poisonous mineral**, gnaw my inwards.

By comparing the thought to a poisonous substance, Iago emphasises how it physically pains him, eating him up inside.

Hyperbole
Hyperbole is a Greek word meaning exaggeration for effect.

For example, in *A Midsummer Night's Dream*:

> HELENA
> No, no, I am as **ugly as a bear**,
> For **beasts that meet me run away for fear**.

Here Helena is using hyperbole in comparing herself to a 'bear', to hammer home the point that she thinks she is so ugly no one could possibly love her.

Onomatopoeia
A long and difficult-to-spell word which refers to words that sound like their meaning.

For example, in *The Tempest*:

> CALIBAN
> Sometimes a thousand **twangling** instruments
> Will **hum** about mine ears; and sometime voices

'Twangling' is a made-up word which perfectly describes the sound that Caliban is talking about, because the word itself sounds like it. The word 'hum' is also onomatopoeic because of the 'h' sound which makes you sigh out, and the 'mm' at the end.

Double entendre
A word which has two meanings. Often the second is risqué.

For example, in *As You Like It* when Rosalind, talking about love and marriage, says:

> ROSALIND
> Why then, can one desire too much of a good **thing**?

'Thing' means the same as our modern meaning; *something*, but was also a slang word for *penis*.

3. Character

The first thing to do when approaching a Shakespeare character is to analyse their speech.

Take a Shakespeare monologue, and go through the text highlighting each device from the list above as you find it. Try to highlight each in a different colour, for example:

> Metaphor – highlight yellow

> Antithesis – highlight green
> Strong vowel sounds – highlight blue.

When your page is full of different coloured markings, you will see what extraordinary depths are hidden within. Now, remain curious, playful and aware of this information. I am sure you will notice what depth and colour has been released from the text.

An example character

Let's take an extract of text and look in more detail at how you might go about analysing it. I have chosen a section of *Julius Caesar*, from Act 2, Scene 1. Although the passage is a dialogue between two characters – Portia and Brutus – Brutus' lines are often cut and Portia's lines stitched together by actors who wish to perform it as a monologue.

This is just an example. It is not set in stone and neither is it right nor wrong. These are just some observations from investigating, looking for clues and decoding.

The lines are numbered to help you match up the analysis with the text.

> ***Julius Caesar*
> by William Shakespeare**
>
> *Act 2, Scene 1*
>
> PORTIA
> It will not let you eat, nor talk, nor sleep;   1
> And could it work so much upon your shape   2
> As it hath much prevailed on your condition,   3

I should not know you, Brutus. Dear my lord,	4
Make me acquainted with your cause of grief.	5

BRUTUS
I am not well in health, and that is all.	6

PORTIA
Brutus is wise, and were he not in health,	7
He would embrace the means to come by it.	8

BRUTUS
Why, so I do. Good Portia, go to bed.	9

PORTIA
Is Brutus sick? And is it physical	10
To walk unbracéd and suck up the humours	11
Of the dank morning? What, is Brutus sick?	12
And will he steal out of his wholesome bed	13
To dare the vile contagion of the night?	14
And tempt the rheumy and unpurgéd air	15
To add unto his sickness? No my Brutus,	16
You have some sick offence within your mind	17
Which by the right and virtue of my place	18
I ought to know of: and upon my knees	19
I charm you, by my once commended beauty,	20
By all your vows of love and that great vow	21
Which did incorporate and make us one,	22
That you unfold to me, your self, your half,	23
Why you are heavy, and what men tonight	24
Have had resort to you, for here have been	25
Some six or seven who did hide their faces	26
Even from darkness.	27

> BRUTUS
> Kneel not, gentle Portia. 28
>
> PORTIA
> I should not need, if you were gentle Brutus. 29
> Within the bond of marriage, tell me, Brutus, 30
> Is it excepted I should know no secrets 31
> That appertain to you? Am I your self 32
> But as it were in sort or limitation? 33
> To keep with you at meals, comfort your bed, 34
> And talk to you sometimes? Dwell I but in the
> suburbs 35
> Of your good pleasure? If it be no more 36
> Portia is Brutus' harlot, not his wife. 37

Research

Plot

Julius Caesar is set in Rome, in 44 BC.
There is a conspiracy against the Roman Emperor Julius Caesar.
Portia is married to the protagonist of the play, Marcus Brutus, who is conspiring to kill Caesar.

What's happening in the scene?

In the small hours of the morning, Portia, unable to sleep, has got out of bed to find out where her husband is. She decides to confront him about his behaviour. She has witnessed his recent distress and is trying to get him to open up to her about what is going on. The conspiracy, betrayal, and the incompatibility of these events against his political ideals, is stressing Brutus out. He's tortured by the question of what course of action is best for the Roman Empire and this is dramatically changing his personality.

Brutus has become completely unrecognisable to Portia. He is changed, distant and hurting her. Portia feels rejected and marginalised from a man she loves, a man whom she has been married to for some time.

At this point Portia has gone so far as to self-harm to demonstrate the strength of her desire for answers from her husband: she says later in the scene that she has wounded herself in the thigh as a 'proof' of her 'constancy'. She's unable to continue this internal torture. She needs an explanation now.

Does Portia know what Brutus is planning to do? What are her suspicions?

Later in the play, despairing due to Brutus' lengthy absence and the increased strength and power of Mark Antony and Octavius, Portia commits suicide by eating burning coals.

Who is Portia?
Detective work will tell you that Portia is the educated daughter of the Roman army general Cato. She has status in her own right. She is also equal in intelligence to her husband.

> PORTIA
> [Aside] O constancy, be strong upon my side:
> Set a huge mountain 'tween my heart and tongue.
> I have a man's mind, but a woman's might.
> (*Act 2, Scene 4*)

Her eloquent heart-felt speech reflects all of this, and her self-harm presents another aspect of her character.

Turn to page 115 for a walk-through of the detailed approach to researching a character. Use some of these strategies to help you to discover Portia.

What about the text?

This extract is all in **verse**.

See how Portia generally follows the iambic pentameter, with ten syllables in most of her lines. This might show that despite her anguish, Portia is in control of her thoughts and she is mindful at all times of the need to stop Brutus from walking away. Should she anger him, all is lost.

Some lines, such as 29, 30 and 35, have extra syllables. Notice what Portia is saying in these lines. Also notice how Portia overruns the meter with increasing frequency as the scene develops. Why might that be? Can we see her growing frustration through verse here?

Notice in line 1 the **vowel** sounds that express deep emotion.

> '*It will not let you **ea**t, n**or** t**a**lk, n**or** sl**ee**p*'
>   eee   oor oor   oor eee

Say these long vowel sounds out loud. See how they connect with your diaphragm and sit at the very pit of your stomach. Vowels are open channels, they access what is raw inside your belly and they often depict emotion.

The words create the emotion in themselves – you don't have to add emotion on top, just feel it inside.

Line 1, '*It will not let you eat, nor talk, nor sleep'*, is also the first example of **a list of three**, making a strong punchy argument.

At Line 3 we see percussive **consonants** picking up as the piece drives forward to Portia's first conclusion:

> '**A*s*** *i**t** **h**a**th** **m**u**ch** **pr**e**v**ai**l**e**d** o**n** **y**our **c**on**d**i**t**io**n**'
>   z t h th m ch pr v l d n y   c nd sh n

These consonants give the text a more crisp and factual delivery as Portia speaks her mind.

In line 4, Portia returns to open emotional vowel sounds to conclude:

> '***I*** sh**ou**ld n**o**t kn**ow** y**ou**, Br**u**t**u**s.'
> ayy oo   o   ohh oo   oo uh

Portia then states her **objective** outright:

> '*Make me acquainted with your cause of grief.*'

Part Two: Your Skills

Brutus deflects, saying he is not well and telling Portia to go to bed.

Portia contends with Brutus, using logic to deliver an argument through a series of **rhetorical questions** over lines 10–16 that prove Brutus is not sick.

Look at the **punctuation** – the question marks in this section appear often in the middle of lines, so that there is a **caesura** and then Portia moves straight on to another point. The **enjambment** speeds up her stream of questions as she makes her point. She argues that if Brutus were physically sick, he would not walk about outside in the cold night making his illness worse.

Portia repeats the word 'sick', with its hissing 's' and hard 'ck' throughout this section, then plays on its meaning in line 17 (after the caesura in line 16 and the strong, definite 'N**o**, m**y** Br**u**t**u**s'):

> 'You have some **sick** offence within your mind
> Which by the right and virtue of my place
> I ought to know of'

It is not Brutus who is 'sick', she argues, but the 'offence' that he is planning, and by the right and virtue of her marriage to him and place in the world she should be told what is going on.

Right and virtue are two separate points.

- *Virtue* is conforming to and carrying out moral and ethical principles.

161

- *Right* is an entitlement, that Portia has as Brutus' wife. It also reminds Brutus that Portia is a lady with rank in her own right.

How difficult might it be to tell your husband that he is sick in the mind without him walking off?

Finally, Portia uses the last tool left to her – she begs Brutus on her knees (line 19).

Kneeling was a powerful gesture in Shakepeare's time, and is a trump card here for Portia. Remember that the wound to her thigh may be even more painful as she kneels.

> Line 19
> ...*and upon my knees*
> I charm you by my once commended beauty,
> By all your vows of love, and that great vow
> Which did incorporate and make us one,
> That you unfold to me, your self, your half,
> Why you are heavy, and what men tonight
> Have had resort to you, for here have been
> Some six or seven, who did hide their faces
> Even from darkness.

When kneeling, Portia tries a new strategy, reminiscing about their past romance. She reminds Brutus how beautiful he once said she was, and how constantly loving he used to be to her.

She returns to the powerful **list of three** in *'to me, your self, your half'*, but still getting nothing from Brutus, Portia confronts him with what she knows – that a group of men have been to their home to see him, and that their mission was of such importance they felt it necessary to hide their faces... even in the dead of night. Yet still Brutus does not give in. He asks her not to kneel.

> Line 29
> *I should not need, if you were gentle Brutus.*
> *Within the bond of marriage, tell me, Brutus,*
> *Is it excepted I should know no secrets*
> *That appertain to you? Am I your self*
> *But as it were in sort or limitation?*
> *To keep with you at meals, comfort your bed*
> *And talk to you sometimes? Dwell I but in the suburbs*
> *Of your good pleasure? If it be no more,*
> *Portia is Brutus' harlot, not his wife.*

Portia turns Brutus' 'gentle' back to him. (Remember to listen to (or to read) the lines of the other characters, so as to pick up on moments like this where words are repeated between speakers). She replies that she would not have to kneel if *he* were 'gentle'; if he were considerate of her feelings.

She then reminds him of their marriage vows, that it is her duty as his wife to know what is troubling him. She asks several more **rhetorical questions**, and uses another **list of three** when she describes her reduced role as a wife as being *'To keep with you at meals, comfort your bed / And talk to you sometimes'*.

Notice also that this list of three revisits Brutus' symptoms from the beginning of the monologue ('It will not let you eat, nor talk, nor sleep').

Finally, Portia goes as far as to describe herself as a harlot – this perhaps reveals Portia's disgust at herself as well as her husband. It is a last-ditch attempt to get Brutus to tell her what is wrong.

These are just some detective work avenues to explore.

What do YOU notice about this piece of writing? Remember:

Portia must have a clear **objective**, e.g.

> 'I must get you to tell me what's wrong, NOW or I shall end my life with this torment.'

She needs an **internal obstacle** to overcome:

> 'The emotional cost this is having on me is making me ill.'

She has an **external obstacle** to overcome:

> Brutus' obstinacy.

What are the **stakes** here?

> 'If I don't handle this well, he will walk away, and our marriage will be a sham. I'll return to despair, and I may as well kill myself.'

Some final maxims in preparing any Shakespeare text

1. **Take the thought to the end of the phrase.**
   A thought propels us to speak. In Shakespeare's plays, characters can have very long thoughts. They can be four or five lines long, and full of commas and colons, etc., but they continue on to the full stop. Of course you can pause or breathe within a thought, but it must carry on believably.
   It's important not to drop the energy at the end of the thought. It is a springboard for your next thought, so keep the energy up and drive on through.
2. **Don't be afraid of the text.**
   Research, explore, mull over all sorts of ideas unique to you; different theories, contexts, line readings, different reactions, different impulses and different reasons for why you say what you say.
3. **The emotion and the truth comes from the thoughts you think and the words you speak.**
   In this speech, Portia's focus is on Brutus – not on herself. You are not here to do anything but speak the words and work through the thought processes. Desperate emotive cries, tears and gasps are NOT what is required. If they are appropriate and truthful, they will come naturally.

Sight-reading

Sight-reading can be particularly challenging for dyslexic actors, and while it is something which can be asked of you in an audition, you or your agent should always ask for any material in advance so that you can be allowed to prepare.

Note: You may be nervous about telling a potential employer that you are dyslexic. It's important to remember that it is illegal for anyone to choose *not* to give you a job for this reason. You might not get the job for other reasons but you should feel able to share this information about yourself comfortably so that you can ask for the support you need to do your best in auditions and rehearsals.

In the case of a first read-through of a play in rehearsals, you should have done all your preparation of the text in advance, and so you will not really be sight-reading (see the 'Text' section from page 79 to learn more about this process). However, to give you confidence in that out-loud read-through, you can still prepare by doing the following:

Goals and obstacles

Goal
To be able to read a text you've never seen before fluently and calmly in a way that can be understood by your audience.

Obstacles
- Nerves
- Unfamiliar words
- Moving text (for those who experience this)
- Processing speed.

Strategies

1. Make use of access tools

What is it?
There are certain practical things that can be done with text to make it easier to read.

If you know what supports you best, you and/or your agent can ask for these things to be provided by the director or casting director.

Alternatively, there are tools which you can make or buy to help you, and you might like to take those with you into a situation where you might be asked to sight-read.

Why is it useful?
Lots of research has been put into finding ways to support dyslexic actors, and while your needs are individual, they may well be helped by things which have also helped other people.

How do I do it?
- You can ask for material to be printed in a particular font. Try some simple fonts such as Arial or Open Sans (the font used throughout this book), in point sizes that aren't too small (such as size 12).
- You can ask for any material you will need to sight-read to be provided on coloured paper.
   - Go and buy a pack of different coloured paper, and experiment with printing things on the different colours. Is there a colour that makes text easier to read for you?

- ○ If you are uncomfortable with asking for this in advance, you can help yourself by buying a coloured overlay – this is a see-through coloured film that you can place over white paper to make the print clearer.
- You can also purchase or make guided reading strips – these are strips of paper or card with a hole cut out so that you can only see the line you are reading, and you move the strip down the page, sentence by sentence or line by line. This will help you to focus on the bit you are reading.

These tools are easy to purchase online, just do a web search.

If you don't want to use any of these methods, simply use your finger as a marker. With one hand holding the script, you can use the other to mark the line you are reading with a pointed finger or a horizontal finger sliding down the page like a ruler.

2. Re-focus your attention

What is it?
Taking your attention off yourself and putting it on the text, or on the other person in the scene.

Why is it useful?
One of the biggest barriers to successful sight-reading for dyslexic actors is being distracted by your own panic. If you are focused on the text you cannot focus on yourself.

How do I do it?
Turn your thinking away from yourself and onto the text. The writer wrote it for the audience – you are just the vessel of transportation. It's not about YOU. Once you stop focusing on yourself, you'll find connecting with the text a lot easier.

Realise that weeks of work goes into a performance. This sight-reading cannot possibly match that, and whoever you are sight-reading to knows this! If you alter your attitude and see this as an 'offering' to begin from, you might feel freer. Remember they aren't looking for perfection, but for a bold, interesting choice, and potential.

3. Practise  M

What is it?
Practising at home in your own time.

Why is it useful?
The more you practise sight-reading, the better you will get at it. Sight-reading will become more habitual and less scary, and instead of panicking when you get asked to sight-read, you'll know what to do – you'll have already done it loads of times!

How do I do it?
- Practise little and often: Do a workout every day if you can – this makes for mastery.
- Try sight-reading five lines of one column in a newspaper.

- Try with an old script or a book.
- Now try an advert, or cooking instructions on food. Anything is practice!

As you get better, try to raise your head from the text more often, so that when you are reading for an audience they get to see your eyes and not only the top of your head.

Read through the first thought looking down at the text. Then raise your head and eyeline to speak the line to the other actor(s). Then look down to read the next thought, and up again to speak it, and so on.

This process may feel quite slow, but don't worry, as long as you are holding the attention of the audience with your delivery, they will wait.

4. Read actively

What is it?
In most situations where you are required to sight-read you should still be given the opportunity to read over the text briefly before you 'perform' it. In an audition, you may have a few minutes outside the room with the text before you go in. If you are handed the text in the audition you can request this preparation time.

This strategy is about physicalising the text in your practice read-through.

Why is it useful?
It will help you to absorb and understand the information in the text as you read over it. It will also focus you and

force you to be active, which will make it harder for you to be distracted by panic and simply run your eyes over the text without taking any of it in.

How do I do it?
1. Read the text aloud slowly (including the stage directions and scene settings – these contain helpful clues)
2. Use one or several of the first six strategies listed below, under 'Line-absorbing'. They run from page 171 to page 182.

As you are likely to be short on time, use whichever exercises work best for you, but if you can, try a combination of several. It is like building up a wall from different layers of bricks, one layer at a time to take you to a position of knowing more than you did in the beginning.

Line-absorbing

Naturally, the pressure of remembering lines, when they can easily disappear, is challenging. This pressure in the space can lead to anxiety and tension – in the body and mind. So you must move beyond this: connect your text and your body, and TRUST yourself and the work you've done.

Don't worry about 'remembering'. Instead of 'learning lines', think of this process as 'absorbing' what your character says. Line-learning is about using your senses to take the words from your brain into your body until you embody the text.

Things that may help include:
- Learning small chunks at a time
- Repetition
- Using all your senses: seeing, tasting, hearing, touching and smelling.

Seeing, hearing, doing, chanting, imagining, touching and moving with the words will embed them inside you.

I know dyslexic actors who still like to write lines out by hand. If this helps you, go for it! But until you try out these other methods too, you won't know what suits you best. No one else knows how *your* brain best holds on to information, but the best chance you can give it is to offer it different ways of doing so, and to try layer after layer of different exercises to see what sticks.

Imagine that for every one of these techniques you develop, you grow roots into the earth. You will, by the end of the exercises, be firmly rooted with solid knowledge inside you.

The line-absorbing/learning exercises below are suggestions to try, that allow your senses and your body to work to support your brain. Over time, you can alter them to suit you.

Part Two: Your Skills

Goals and obstacles

Goal
To be able to learn lines efficiently and reliably.

Obstacles
- Poor memory
- Slow processing
- Not knowing how to go about it.

Strategies

Note: As well as being useful to help you learn your lines, the first six of these strategies can be used as quick techniques to approach a piece of text that you have to sight-read. For more on sight-reading, turn to page 165.

1. Physicalising the punctuation  N

What is it?
This exercise examines the punctuation to help you make sense of the text you are speaking.

Why is it useful?
If your phonic awareness (awareness of how words sound) is challenged, it will be trickier for you to understand the sense of a text. This exercise will really help you. It slows the text down to a speed you can speak and understand it.

The Dyslexic Actor

How do I do it?

Pick a section of your text. It could be a monologue or a scene with lots of people speaking in it.

Mark the end of every sentence with a slash using a pencil.

Here is an example from *Two Billion Beats* by Sonali Bhattacharyya (Scene 3, page 33):

> I mean, Mum's talking to me again, yeah? / *Really* talking to me. / Telling me stuff I've never known before. / So what am I supposed to do? / She told me about this friend she had, growing up. / Her best friend. / Mariam.

Now read the text aloud slowly and clearly, without trying to act.

How was that? Did you understand more of it?

Now we're moving up a gear!

You're going to read the text again clearly and slowly, but this time at every comma in the text: (,) *click your fingers.*

At every full stop (.) question mark (?) and exclamation mark (!) *slap your thigh.*

Do this more slowly than feels comfortable, for the entire text you are wanting to absorb.

> **Remember!** Slow and focused is good. Notice the sense of the sentence as you read it. Have you

> understood what you've read? If you go slowly and do this, you will be surprised how the sense springs to mind.

2. Separate the thoughts

What is it?
This exercise helps you figure out the thoughts behind the text.

Why is it useful?
If we fear words, we can be tempted to rush through text to get it over with quickly. Please don't! Separating your thoughts is very useful, and helps you get to grips with your character's psychology, as well as connecting you to the words, helping you to remember them.

How do I do it?
Take a pen, and on the page mark the different thoughts with a coloured slash. The thought might be the length of a sentence, it might be shorter than a sentence, or run over two sentences.

If our text is this example from *Two Billion Beats* by Sonali Bhattacharyya again:

> I mean, Mum's talking to me again, yeah? *Really* talking to me. Telling me stuff I've never known before. So what am I supposed to do? She told me about this friend she had, growing up. Her best friend. Mariam.

the thoughts could be:

> I mean, Mum's talking to me again, yeah? *Really* talking to me. / Telling me stuff I've never known before. / So what am I supposed to do? / She told me about this friend she had, growing up. Her best friend. Mariam.

You can also re-type the thoughts on your laptop.

Type each line of text.

Break it up like this.

This clearly shows your new thoughts.

Here is another new thought.

For example:

> I mean, Mum's talking to me again, yeah? *Really* talking to me.
>
> Telling me stuff I've never known before.
>
> So what am I supposed to do?
>
> She told me about this friend she had, growing up. Her best friend. Mariam.

If you re-type the text, putting each thought on a new line, this clearly shows you different things to say, in a visible list going down the page, rather than in a dense paragraph.

Speak the first thought slowly. When you have got to grips with thought 1, move on to thought 2 and go through the same process.

3. Exaggerators

What is it?
This exercise focuses on exaggerated facial movements.

Why is it useful?
You want to be able to deliver free-flowing fluent text, so you need to absorb information in a way that means it trips off the tongue. This exercise gives your face, your mouth, lips, tongue and jaw a chance to build muscle memory.

How do I do it?
Read the text, exaggerating your facial movements as you speak slowly.

Make weird faces as you say each word, slowly flexing your mouth as much as possible.

Do this again, and notice both the cumbersome words and those words that flow more easily.

Try to involve *all* your facial muscles.

Now repeat on a whisper.

Move towards a fast delivery.

Notice the journey your body goes on, and play, until a familiar fluency begins to happen.

From here you can move with your text learning to…

4. Articulators

 o

What is it?
Exaggerating your use of your articulators as you pronounce your lines, to help you remember them.

Your main articulators are your tongue, your upper lip, your lower lip, your upper teeth, your upper gum ridge (alveolar ridge), your hard palate, your soft palate (velum), your uvula (the free-hanging end of the soft palate), your pharyngeal wall, and your glottis (the space between your vocal folds).

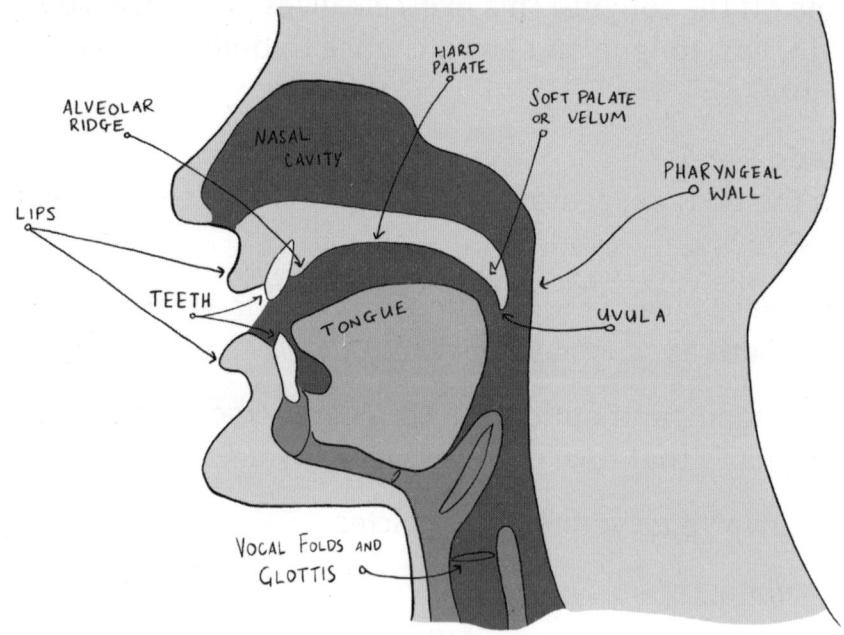

Why is it useful?
Exaggerating the use of your articulators will help you remember text patterns.

How do I do it?
Slowly say: 'The lips, the teeth, the tip of the tongue and the hard palate.' You've just used your articulators! Warming them up with phrases like this allows you to move more fluently through the words.

Once you've got all your articulators working, your text will flow. It will be clearer and more distinct. If the words flow more easily you will hear them more comprehensibly and remember them more effectively.

Say one of your lines.

Notice how the words feel in your mouth.

Your tongue is an overworked and under-appreciated muscle. So much relies on it.

Notice what it does and how it is supported by other articulators.

Having played with the text, exaggerating and articulating, reflect on whether muscle memory has begun to kick in. Try saying one of your lines without having it written in front of you. Has this helped?

5. Gestures  P

What is it?
Using hand gestures to help embed the text in your physical memory.

Why is it useful?
Research proves that gesturing leads to better recall.

Gestures are our body's way of communicating. We use gestures all the time to help explain what we want to say. This exercise allows you to get the words into your body through gesture. It doesn't matter what gesture you choose to depict a thought or tricky word – the fact is, if you repeat the gesture again and again as a strategy for remembering, the gesture will help.

How do I do it?
Place your script on a table or stick it to a wall.

Take a line of your script.

For example, take the line, *'I love you very much, George.'*

I say the first word *'I'*, and I point to myself.

I then say the word *'love'*, and I gesture to my heart.

I then say *'you'*, and point to George.

I say *'very much'* and my gesture might be holding my arms out wide.

I say *'George'*, and point to George again.

The gestures could also be more abstract, a gesture that summarises that certain word to you.

For example, *'O for a muse of fire that would ascend the brightest heaven of invention'*

O:	making an O with fingers.
Muse:	hands creating a beautiful woman's curved body.

> *Fire:* fingers flickering like a fire.
> *Ascend*: hand going upwards, lifting.
> *Brightest:* hands making firework fingers, flashing.
> *Heaven:* stretch tall.

It doesn't matter what the gesture is so long as you repeat the same gesture each time you speak the line. Don't think about what the gesture should be: be instinctive, be larger than life, be playful.

6. Pictures for words

What is it?
Translating your script into pictures.

Why is it useful?
This strategy is simply a different notation process from letters and words. This is a useful technique for visual learners, and for tapping into creative curiosity, as well as thinking outside the box. The actor Lloyd Everitt, the youngest actor to have played Othello at the Globe Theatre, is dyslexic. He uses this method, as do many other successful actors, for memory recall.

How do I do it?
Draw pictures to represent the words of your text, quickly and without too much thought.

It is useful to draw the same image each time the same word appears, so the brain can recognise it quickly.

For example:

Then, speak the text whilst looking at the images.

Assess how many symbols you need to remember a phrase. You certainly shouldn't need a picture for every single word.

7. Snowballing

What is it?
A snowball starts off as a small ball, but when you roll it more snow gathers, and it gets bigger and bigger. Snowballing builds your learning incrementally. You learn one bit of text, then the next, and the next and the next.

Why is it useful?
This method works well because you're becoming aware of what you are remembering and able to see progress, giving you the confidence to keep going.

How do I do it?
Take a line of your text.

For example:

> It will not let you eat, nor talk, nor sleep; And could it work so much upon your shape, As it hath much prevailed on your condition...

Read the first part of the phrase:

> It will not let you eat

Now say it without looking.

Then read the first bit of the phrase and add a little more:

> It will not let you eat, nor talk

Now say that section without looking.

Now read the phrase, again from the beginning, adding a bit more:

> It will not let you eat, nor talk, nor sleep

Then say it without looking, and so on.

8. Furniture Post-its  Q

What is it?
The dyslexic actress Kara Tointon, who played Olivia in *Twelfth Night* for the Royal Shakespeare Company in 2018, and filmed the dyslexic programme 'Don't call me stupid',

raised valuable awareness of the challenges of memory recall, as well as processing issues. One of the techniques she liked was furniture Post-its. It suited her way of being physical in the space.

Why is it useful?
Signs placed on different objects or furniture around the room create a great prompt and keep you active in the space. Object to word associations work well with the dyslexic strength of association. This is visual memory working to its benefit. The change of direction, and movement required to move towards each piece of furniture, forms a geographical pattern associated with the words. Your ears are hearing, your mouth muscles delivering the text, and several senses are jointly engaged to give your brain the best chance.

How do I do it?
Let's assume you are tackling ten lines of text. Bring ten objects or items of furniture such as chairs, tables, and stools into the area you want to work in. Space them randomly around the room. You might want to use items relevant to the text – for example, in a kitchen scene, use a glass, spoon, etc.

Decide how you want to transfer the text onto Post-its. It might be your whole line, it might be an image to prompt your line, or it might be the particular word or words within the line that you are struggling to recall or get right. If you choose to draw pictures, the work that goes into drawing the images offers a means of addressing the lines in detail.

You will begin this exercise with your script in hand, but with time and repetition you will be able to put that down and work only with the Post-it prompts.

Stick your ten Post-its on your ten objects.

From a chosen starting point, walk towards the first piece of furniture/object as you speak your first line aloud.

Touch the object as you arrive, to establish its presence.

Speak the second line while walking to the next piece of furniture. The third line to the next, and so on, until ten lines have been spoken to different objects. Repeat again, walking to the furniture in the same order as before.

The first big achievement will be putting down the script that's in your hand – but you'll still have the prompts on the Post-its to help you. If you began with the full text written on the Post-its, eventually you should be able to have just one word or an image on each.

9. Last-word repeater

What is it?
Repeating the last word of the previous line: either your previous sentence, or the other character's line, and adding it to the front of the sentence you are going to speak.

Why is it useful?
Repeating the last word of the previous idea is a great prompt to make sure you are actively listening, and it helps you find out what triggers your desire to speak.

How do I do it?
Go through the text adding the last word of the previous sentence to the beginning of your own sentence. Now say it and follow on with your line. This can work for a monologue or duologue.

10. Trigger word

What is it?
The idea here is to choose a trigger word said by the person speaking to you, to use that to prompt your next thought.

Why is it useful?
This exercise helps you to specify your thoughts, and to make them directly linked to the things being said to you – this will add truthfulness but also make your lines easier to remember.

How do I do it?
Take your scene partner's lines and decide on trigger words in their cues that prompt you to speak.

Here is an example from *Imperium: The Cicero Plays* adapted by Mike Poulton from Robert Harris's novels (*Caesar*, Scene 2):

> CAESAR. Aha! A politician's answer! You should write your memoirs, you know.
>
> CICERO. Perhaps.
>
> CAESAR. But you'll let me glance through them before you publish, won't you?
>
> CICERO. I'd be honoured.

If you are playing Cicero, the trigger word you choose from Caesar's first line might be MEMOIRS. 'Memoirs' is the trigger word that prompts your response 'Perhaps'. You can choose any word.

In the next exchange, you might choose 'publish' as a trigger to remind you of your next line, 'I'd be honoured'. When you hear 'publish' you know what your reaction should be.

This is useful when getting familiar with the dialogue in the early stages of learning. It is not a substitute for listening to your fellow actor's entire line.

11. Did I get that?

What is it?
In this exercise you tune into what the person before you has said by repeating out their lines.

Why is it useful?
As a dyslexic actor, speaking aloud and repeating back allows you to process, and very importantly to understand

what they are saying to you. It also helps trigger your reaction.

How do I do it?
Take your scene partner's line – the one before you speak.

Speak their line out loud.

Then say out loud 'Did I get that?'

Then say your own line.

12. Ear ear

What is it?
Recording the text and listening to it in order to absorb it.

Why is it useful?
It encourages you to listen actively.

How do I do it?
Record the text you want to absorb, slowly and clearly in a bland voice. This stops specific line reading patterns forming in your brain, allowing you to absorb the words, but to offer different deliveries/reactions. If it is a duologue, record the text you will be reacting to (your scene partner's lines), as well as your own lines.

Then blindfold yourself or close your eyes and play the recording.

Listen and actively engage with what you are hearing. Do any images come to mind? Do these images form a pattern or a journey? Do any sensations, colours, smells, feelings, words or shapes come to mind? When hearing your scene partner's lines, do you want to react?

Listen to it again. And again. Do any of the words seem to be sticking?

Have a go and see if you can speak with and over your recorded lines at the same time.

Now turn off the recording. Can you speak a version of what you can remember with your eyes closed? You can lie down or move in the space – whatever feels comfortable.

13. Memory house

What is it?
A way of remembering facts by associating them with a journey or room in a home.

Why is it useful?
The late Professor Stephen Hawking spoke of using this at night when he had no means of recording or writing down his thoughts and ideas. It may be useful for you if you have strong skills of imagination to harness a line of text to a room in a house in your mind.

How do I do it?
Take a line from your script and place it in a room in your imagination. Use a room that is familiar to you, in a building with other rooms that are familiar to you. Go on doing this with other lines and rooms. When you

are running your lines, move from room to room in the building in your head while you say them.

This is sometimes useful if you want to work on your lines while on a journey where chanting aloud and moving in the space isn't possible. For example, on a two-hour train journey. If you have a strong imagination, discipline, and determination not to be distracted, give it a try.

As an alternative to attaching lines to an imaginary room in a house, you can do it directly with objects in the room you are actually in. If you are on a train, for example, you can notice what is around you and attach lines to the:

- Luggage rack
- Clock
- Exit sign
- Window
- Headrest in front, etc.

Anything in your vision will work, if you attach one line of text to each object.

Have the text on your lap. Keep focussed and read the line and repeat it looking at the object (in reality or in your mind). Read the line of text again and repeat it looking at the object. Snowball this process by adding line after line and repeating. Be sure to always look again at the object associated to the line. Linking words and associations might be a strength you didn't know you had. You may have a knack of hunting out objects that seem to go with the line of text.

14. Mime magic

What is it?
The idea of this exercise is to improvise and mime to the recorded text of your dialogue, in order to embody the text.

Why is it useful?
This allows you to devote all your energy to embodying your movement, with full focus on the words you are hearing. This exercise brings energy into your body that may add to your processing of the words and to your chosen characterisation. You will also absorb what you are listening to, and it will begin to sink in.

How do I do it?
1. Record your dialogue.
2. Go into a space, play the recording aloud and begin to improvise gestures to mime the lines *without speaking*.
3. Continue listening to the text, adding gestures.
4. Repeat, but now saying the lines aloud while doing the gestures.
5. Continue to repeat, and the gestures should help to make the lines feel more familiar.

15. Line-learning apps

What is it?
Download an app to your phone or tablet which is designed to help with the process of learning lines.

Why is it useful?

Line-learning apps have the edge on a straight-through recording you might make of any dialogue because they are programmed to be able to remove your lines but leave a space of the right length between your scene partner's lines, to allow you to practise saying your own.

This saves you needing to ask other people to test you and means that you can practise any time, even on the move.

How do I do it?

There are a number of apps available, some of them are free. Do a search on the internet and try some out to see what works for you.

Part Three: Your Career

Auditioning

Auditions are the day-to-day life of an actor, and you will, of course, get many more auditions than parts, so you need to learn to embrace them.

No one delivers an out-of-the-box outcome like a dyslexic person. The challenge is keeping this at the front of your mind as you try to overcome some commonly found dyslexic obstacles. This section will help you do that, so you can deliver your best performance in the audition room and build your strength and resilience as an actor.

The strategies which follow are about giving you control over auditioning as best as you can. However, awareness in the arts of what dyslexia really is – of its strengths and challenges – is gradually getting better. Venues, directors and casting directors are becoming more aware of how they can support dyslexic actors, so speak up if you're struggling with something, they can help you.

> To read more about what support you can ask for, turn to page 167.

> ## Goals and obstacles
>
> ### Goals
> - To be offered roles
> - To feel as if you did a good job
> - To know you are enough.
>
> ### Obstacles
> - A lack of confidence
> - Nerves
> - Burying your head in the sand
> - Organisation
> - Challenges with:
>   - memorising lines
>   - bringing a prepared script off the page
>   - sight reading
>   - managing recovery after an audition.

Planning for the audition

Strategies

1. Start at the very beginning: know yourself

What is it?
To feel comfortable with, and even enjoy, auditions, as with all things, the best and only place to start from is YOURSELF. You must analyse and learn from your triumphs and your mistakes.

Why is it useful?
A dyslexic person works in unique ways. It's your job to find out what those ways are for you, so that you can put in place the right tools for you to succeed in an audition.

How do I do it?
Grab a pen and paper or a laptop to type on.

Ask yourself:
- Do I have previous feelings about/experience of auditions?
- What went well last time?
- What didn't work so well?
- What did I learn from this? What would I do differently next time?
- Was I disciplined in my preparation?
- Did I become distracted/did anything interfere with my focus?
- Was I interested and excited about what I had to do?
- Did I set myself a realistic time frame?
- Did I enjoy any part of the process? If so, why?

Have a look over your answers; notice the areas that need more work. This is an invaluable base from which to improve.

Now ask yourself some more general questions about how you interact in situations such as auditions. You might have learned strategic protection skills that you may or may not even be aware of. Do you recognise any of the following behaviours in yourself?:

- Deciding never to ask questions
- Never admitting you don't understand
- Wanting to say the right thing, to please others
- Forming a mask to hide behind or a bubble to exist in
- Covering up pain, and lying
- Not looking people in the eye, to avoid being questioned.

Forgive yourself for these habits, if you recognise them, but decide to work against them too. They aren't helping you.

Finally, think of this audition as another opportunity to learn more about yourself and your process, so that each time you become even better prepared for the next.

2. Realign your mindset regarding auditions

What is it?
Changing your mindset to one that:
- Knows you're capable
- Doesn't take itself too seriously
- Embraces your dyslexic strengths
- Isn't afraid or thrown by making mistakes.

Why is it useful?
Because if you go into an audition hopeful – full of optimism and possibility – you are much more likely to do well and, importantly, to enjoy yourself.

How do I do it?
Remind yourself of the following facts:

- You've been selected to audition because the most basic aspects of who you are: your age, gender, look and energy, link on some level with the character being cast. You're therefore over a huge hurdle before you even start.
- The panel wants to cast you in the role – because then their job is done. They are on your team, and they want you to do well.
- Sometimes what an audition panel are looking for in an actor/character is very fluid. And even when a director *does* have a clear idea of what they are looking for, you might easily bring something which expands or entirely challenges their idea of the character. There is no value in second-guessing – the best thing you can bring is your own personal interpretation.
- The audition room is the *starting place for rehearsal*. You are not expected to bring the final performance in with you.
- No one cares if you mispronounce a name or trip up and re-run a thought. This shows who you are and gives an honest picture of your mannerisms and wonderful glimpses of your true self. Mistakes can create fantastic moments.
- The voice inside you is NOT what the panel are seeing. They have you in front of them demonstrating courage, talent and commitment, so live in this knowledge and leave behind your nerves and insecurities.

3. Build your self-esteem and resilience

What is it?
Yes, you are an actor, and so you perform in front of people with confidence and talent. But you may not feel confident and talented inside.

It can be a frightening and bewildering experience to move through a world where the simplest of day-to-day tasks are confusing. And this is compounded by the fact that few people understand – and you are unable to explain – how it feels.

However, we grow through nurture, kindness, positivity and encouragement. From this position we explore, achieve, fail, reflect and learn.

So you must offer yourself these things. Build up your self-belief and your self-esteem, and you will build up your resilience in the process.

Why is it useful?
A lack of self-esteem cripples the actor in the audition process. By building your self-belief and your resilience you will leave yourself free to play, have fun and explore the character.

How do I do it?

Generally
- Get to know who you are, and get to like yourself. Revisit the things you created in your Identity strategies in Part One: Your Achievements List, your Jelly Person (and Friends), and your Honest Heart.

Part Three: Your Career

> Turn to page 21 to remind yourself of these strategies.

- Be kind to yourself: find solutions, not problems.
- Be kind to others. It makes you feel fantastic.
- Exercise your body. A strong physique offers the best chance of strong self-esteem, and exercise sends lots of happy hormones and chemicals around your body when you do it, too.

Ahead of your audition
- Do your prep – then you will feel ready, full of ideas and pumping to audition.

> The next strategy is all about the preparation you can do.

When the day comes
- Wear your favourite clothes to audition in (and make sure they are clean!) This will help boost your self-confidence going in.
- Think of a colour that makes you feel amazing. Imagine this colour wrapping you up as you practise.

4. Manage your preparation time

What is it?
So you've got a certain amount of time to prepare for an audition. There is a paradox about the dyslexic character that means it's possible you might lean towards one of two extremes:

- You may be frozen by the enormity of the task, and so do nothing, as you don't know where to start,

or

- You might propel yourself through the 48 hours that you have to work on the sides (pages of audition script), and obsessively grind yourself into the ground.

Poor time management can lead to either of these options, so it is important to understand time, and to use it sensibly in order to prepare.

Why is it useful?
Being able to prepare properly is essential to auditioning well. It will empower you and make you feel confident, so that all you have left are healthy nerves and a chance to enjoy your audition.

Learning how to manage your time will give you the best chance of success in this preparation.

How do I do it?
1. Firstly, figure out what kind of audition you're dealing with.
    - Is it for theatre, film, TV, voice over or something else?
    - Do you have to learn the words or just be familiar with them? (Generally for film/TV you are expected to learn the words, whereas for theatre you don't have to.)
    - Do you have to choose your own text for the

Part Three: Your Career

audition, or are you being sent or given sides (some script to work with)?
- Is it a self-tape? If so, do you have a phone/camera and a reading partner?
- If it is in-person, will it just be you and an audition panel, or is it a workshop audition?

Whatever the style of audition, procrastination won't work. It sends you round in spirals of questioning and worry. Be respectful of time. Look for the motivation inside you that says, 'I want to do this, and I want to do it well'.

2. Now, let's assume that there is script for you to prepare. Decide if you are going to audition holding the script and glancing down, or if you are going to be off-book (empty handed).

To help you make this decision, you should work out how much time you have. Sometimes you get the sides sent over a few days in advance; sometimes only the night before! Be realistic about what you can learn and whether learning is necessarily the best way for you to perform well. If there is not enough time to get the script deeply learned, it would be better just to practise it lots and be ready to read it.

> Turn to page 171 for strategies to help you with line-learning, and page 126 for strategies to help you lift the lines off the page when working script-in-hand.

3. You should normally be given at least a little background info about the character, context or plot, but not always. So you need to factor in a sensible amount of time for research, too, to boost your understanding of the role.

Create your own audition checklist
Once you've created this checklist, you will be able to follow it every time, safe in the knowledge that it works for you. Remember if you've got less time, you won't be able to do all the stages: you'll have to choose the most important ones.

Here's an example:

Before the day	
Script research (see page 80 of this book)	☐
Text analysis (see page 90 of this book)	☐
Character work (see page 115 of this book)	☐
Line-learning (see page 171 of this book)	☐
Research details of the company/people I am auditioning for	☐
Eat and drink while preparing	☐
Plan food and water for the day	☐
Get clothes out, clean and ready	☐

Part Three: Your Career

Plan route to audition ☐

Work out timings for arriving calm and prepared ☐

On the day

Wash and dress ☐

Eat ☐

Warm up vocally and physically (see pages 36 and 57 of this book) ☐

Set off on time, so as to arrive ready to do the job ☐

Portion out your time

Be realistic about what you can achieve in the timeframe. If you've only got a day, you've only got a day. What can you get done in this time? How long will it take you to get familiar with the text? How long will it take you to analyse the text and character?

Now create a table for yourself on your computer or by hand:

	Task	Allotted Time	When?	Completed
IN ADVANCE	Script research	2 hours	Mon a.m.	✓
	Text analysis	2.5 hours	Mon p.m.	

	Character	1 hour	Mon p.m.	
	Line-learning	3 hours	Mon p.m. and Tues a.m.	
	Work on delivering the lines freely and creatively	2 hours	Tues p.m.	
	Company research	1 hour	Tues p.m.	
NIGHT BEFORE	Get food/water ready for tomorrow	20mins	Tues evening	
	Put clothes out	20mins	Tues evening	
	Plan route and work out journey timings	30mins	Tues evening	
ON THE DAY	Shower and dress	1 hour	Weds 8 a.m.	
	Eat	30mins	Weds 9 a.m.	
	Do vocal warm-up	30mins	Weds 9:30 a.m.	
	Do physical warm-up	30mins	Weds 10 a.m.	
	Leave home		Weds 10:30 a.m.	

Now go through the checklist, ticking off the stages when you've carried them out.

Working on the audition material

The following five strategies are a speed-through approach to text research, analysis and preparation, reduced to be manageable for audition preparation, when time is short. In addition to these, there are many more strategies available to you in this book if you turn to the chapter on Text, from page 79.

Strategies

1. Be a detective

What is it?
You have been sent sides of script to prepare for the audition. At the beginning, you know nothing. How can you become informed? By becoming a detective and looking for clues in the text to help you figure out what is going on.

Why is it useful?
If you are looking for clues, you will be 'reading actively' – fully focusing on something with a goal. This is great for:
- Focus
- Keeping anxiety away
- Honing your instincts
- Making strong choices for your audition.

How do I do it?
Ask yourself the questions below, and each time you glean some new information, place that image in your mind, or write a word, or draw a picture, to acknowledge the new information.

- What is the title of the play?
- Do you know the author or any of their other works?

- Where is it set?
- What place are you in?
- What time of day is it?
- What is the name of your character?
- Who are you talking and listening to?
- What are your instincts about this person you're talking to?
- Do you listen more or talk more?
- Do you have large chunks of text or one-liners?
- What does this layout say to you?
- Do big chunks show anything?
- Do short one-liners show anything? (an uncomfortable exchange of short pertinent questions? Or crisp consonants relaying a factual rant?)
- What do you want from the other person?
- How can you get what you want? What techniques can you use to get it? Charm? Being demanding?
- What can make the stakes so high that you follow your objective? What will happen if you don't achieve it? What is the possible cost to you?

You can look for:
Relationships – between characters in the scene
Differences – in personalities
Similarities – in personalities.

Remember! There is no right or wrong. You are looking to create a character that's formed on your findings, no one else's. It is your grasp of a character, your courageous choices and your reacting to any text being delivered back to you that is of interest to the panel.

2. Use the punctuation

What is it?
Exploring your text's punctuation to make sense of the text you are speaking.

Why is it useful?
Following the punctuation will help you really understand what is going on.

How do I do it?
Turn to pages 92 and 173 of this book to find exercises on punctuation.

3. Use gestures when you read

What is it?
Physicalising the text with a hand or body gesture.

Why is it useful?
Creating a gesture for a word can slow down your panic and your desire to rush the process, and help you to absorb information. The gesture helps you to 'get the gist' and forces your body and brain to connect.

How do I do it?
Find a place to rest your script. On a window-sill, in your lap, stuck to the wall or on a table. Let's give it a go with these lines from *Jerusalem* by Jez Butterworth (Act 3, page 107):

> 'School is a lie. Prison's a waste of time. Girls are wondrous. Grab your fill. No man was ever lain in his barrow wishing he'd loved one less.'

Now try and think of gestures that conjure each word for you.

e.g.
'School' – a hand writing with a pen
'Is a lie' – a dismissive hand gesture of disgust
'Prison's' – hands shaking the bars of a cell
'Waste' – throwing something into a bin
'Time' – tap watch

At each punctuation mark, stop to take a moment to think about the thought you've just said and gestured. This is to absorb the words within you – you won't make these gestures when you come to do the lines for the audition panel!

4. Last-word repeater

What is it?
Repeating the last word of the previous line before you say your next.

Why is it useful?
It makes sure you are actively listening, and it helps you find out what triggers your desire to speak.

How do I do it?
See page 185 of this book.

5. Reading with images

What is it?
Attaching images to words in your head.

Why is it useful?
Some dyslexic people have the most awesome powers of visualising images in their mind's eye. These are unique to each mind. Images come to mind very quickly, instinctively, and are associated with words that have been read. Images may be associated with past experiences: colours, objects and smells. Imagery can really help you understand and embody text, and it's valuable for line-learning at short notice, too.

This strategy can be especially valuable when confined to a small space where you are unable to get up and move about. A waiting room, queuing, a plane, a train or the car.

How do I do it?
Let's take that *Jerusalem* extract again:

> 'School is a lie. Prison's a waste of time. Girls are wondrous. Grab your fill.'

At every new sentence, take a breath and chant the words slowly. Each breath will calm the mind and might allow a visual picture to come into your memory for the key words and phrases in the sentence. Try it. What do you notice?

- 'School is a lie' – the image might be a classroom from your past, and you might see yourself (as the character) running away from it, to freedom.
- 'Prison's a waste of time' – you might imagine yourself (again, in character) as a bored prisoner sat in a cell.

Read the words aloud again very slowly, in a bland manner. At every comma, full stop, semicolon, ellipses, etc. observe the sense of the thought. Does the image you thought of the first time stay in your mind each time you repeat the sentence?

For a habit to form it takes a good few attempts. However, this will help you to lift the ideas off the page, and also help you to absorb/learn the lines.

> For more techniques to help you learn your lines, turn to page 171.

On the day... and beyond

Strategies

1. Arrive on time and prepared

What is it?
Every person is delayed unavoidably from time to time. A train breaks down, or the traffic is gridlocked. Realistically though, this happens rarely. Have you ever slept through your alarm because you lay awake worrying or running lines? Have you lost your keys when trying to leave on time, or misplaced a shoe?

Very often a dyslexic person picks up the wrong thing; a membership card instead of their bank card, or they can't find the email that was sent with the address because the sender's name doesn't come to mind. It's common to muddle left and right exits from a station, read a word on a sign wrongly, and follow google maps intently to the destination only to find the audition is not there because you typed the address slightly wrongly and are now standing outside the wrong place.

Below are some strategies that will help you manage your time and arrive on time to your audition calm, confident and ready to deliver.

Why is it useful?
Arriving late to the audition makes you look bad, and it also leaves you flustered and unable to do your best work. The point of these strategies is to overcome this. Having done all your prep on time, with everything ready the night before, means there's no need to panic. Time is everything for an actor.

> There is more about managing your time on a day-to-day basis from page 248 of this book.

How do I do it?
Follow your audition checklist (see page 202) – it works! Use alarms and timers to keep yourself on time: for instance, if you've allowed 30 minutes to do your voice warm-up, set a 30-minute timer to keep you on track, and so you can concentrate on warming up properly instead of being distracted worrying about time. If time is short or your audition is particularly early, consider an on-the-go warm-up.

> There are instructions for a time-saving warm-up on page 267 of this book.

Keep your keys, phone and travelcard/ticket in one place: the 'Command Centre' (see page 261), and always put these valuable things there as you arrive home, so they are reliably there the next morning.

Prepare what you need and pack your bag for the next day the night before (audition sides (script), overlay or other tools to help you in the room as a dyslexic actor, water, travel tickets and money). Make sure your phone is charged and your clothes for tomorrow are laid out, washed and ironed.

On the day, monitor who you answer the phone to – it delays you. If you find it hard not to respond to people, and get easily distracted, switch your phone to airplane mode.

Don't get involved with anything other than auditioning (the washing can wait – it will distract you and make you late).

Allow between half an hour and an hour extra for travel delays, because finding the audition place can be hard sometimes. There are apps to show you what a venue looks like and how to find it. Knowing what the building looks like will keep you focused, on track and will save you time.

While you're travelling, concentrate on the route. Without doing so you can easily go on 'auto-pilot', following a typical route you usually take to somewhere else entirely, and only realise this half-way through the trip.

If you're unsure where you're going, and you don't like reading maps and signs, ask someone who obviously has more knowledge than you. The ticket person is likely to know the right train station exit and the road you are looking for. If listening to information is the best way for you to take it in, do it again and again – keep asking.

Some people find navigational apps awkward to work and don't want their phone on show due to the risk of theft. Find your own way and try not to rely solely on having a phone.

Tick your list off as you arrive on time at the venue. It will make you feel empowered and ready for action. Dyslexic actors often worry about remembering things, this is something you didn't have to remember – you just had to follow the list.

And then...

Breathe! Breathing is just about the most important thing in preparing for an audition. Breathing calms you down. Spend 5 minutes taking some time out just to focus on inhaling and exhaling. Take long deep breaths and count out slowly. You can do this at the audition, but also whilst preparing in the days before – whenever is useful for you.

2. Empowerment: owning the room

What is it?
Learning to occupy your space in the audition room with confidence.

Why is it useful?
Low self-esteem can creep up in the room and lead to you not being able to understand instructions from the

panel, or to answer questions. You need to squash that voice that feels inferior in the space. Seeing the space as positive and creative gives a foundation for good acting. It offers you empowerment.

How do I do it?
- Breathe and stand tall.
- Take your time.
- Listen well.
- Be courageous – that means going with your impulses.
- Be accommodating and polite, but also self-assured.
- Enjoy being asked questions, and if you are unclear, be empowered and say so.
- If you need more time, more repetitions, more clarity, speak up. Saying you are dyslexic is not always helpful: this doesn't in itself tell the panel what you need. It is, however, helpful to be specific – say 'Can you repeat that, may I try that again, could I try it slowly first please?'

3. Reading: sight-reading a script

What is it?
Sometimes in an audition you will be asked to read a text you haven't seen beforehand. You'll be given a piece of text from the movie, play, or TV script there and then in the audition room to read immediately.

Sight-reading is an unnatural process as we try to make the words sound familiar, but it is a technique and does improve with practice.

> Find some general strategies for getting more confident with sight-reading by turning to page 165.

Why is it useful?
It's useful for the panel because it allows them to observe you with different text. They can consider options as different ideas circle in their mind.

But you should also therefore see it as useful for you: You might suit this piece of text or role more than the one originally set. You might be considered for a second, different role.

How do I do it?
So, you're at the audition and you've just been given a script to read.

- Ask the panel for a few minutes to prepare your text.
- Slash the text with pencil marks, putting // at the end of each thought or sentence.
- Your sight reading will be easier when you move from // to // rather than seeing a huge dense paragraph of words. These small bite sized chunks are also opportunities to breathe if needed. Breath will calm you and slow your inner rhythm, which can be nervously racing.
- Take a moment to notice which thoughts are questions and which are statements.
- Highlight as necessary.
- If you have tools with you that help, use them: use your coloured overlay, or guided reading strips. Or if

not, just use your finger to mark your way down the page.

> To read more about access tools which may help you, turn to page 167.

Once you're ready to begin, read through the first thought looking down at the text. Then raise your head and eyeline to speak the line to the person reading with you, or to the panel if it's a monologue. Then look down to read the next thought, and up again to speak it, and so on.

Trust your instincts to find the light and shade: make instinctive choices about how to deliver each line, and respond in the moment to what comes from the other person reading in.

4. Recovery: positively moving straight on

What is it?
Focusing on the next thing as soon as you leave the audition.

Why is it useful?
After an audition it is so easy to hold on to the idea of the imperfections you think there were in your interaction or performance, and not to remember the good. You can invent reasons why the panel didn't like you, even though you actually have no idea at all. But life is not just about this audition, so it's essential to be able to move on and put it behind you straight away.

How do I do it?
- Plan something fun to do after your audition. It will relax you, stimulate your creativity and will remind you there is more to life. Have some time off with a friend – you've earned it!
- As you leave the room, forget this project. That casting is over and the next one will be found soon enough. The future is the way forward.
- Unless you have something positive to think about your performance, don't retrace it. You don't know what the panel thought of you, and your perception of yourself is not the one they had of you!
- But DO reflect on what you enjoyed about your process – right through from the planning stages to when you were in the room. What went *well*? You can think about what you might do *differently* when you begin your preparation process next time around.

> The mental resilience required to think in this way can be hard to find sometimes. For advice and strategies to support mental wellbeing, turn to page 225.

Rehearsals

In order to go into rehearsal confidently, you need to do four things first:

- Research – investigate the play

- Analyse the text – find out what clues are there for you
- Consider the character – establish some beliefs about your character from research and text analysis
- Learn lines – embodying the lines within you.

> There are full work-throughs of all of these processes in Part Two: Your Skills from page 33. Turn to the Contents (page vi) to find specific page numbers for each section.

All this preparation will put you in the best possible position for the first day of rehearsals.

However, being dyslexic in a rehearsal room can still be daunting in a particular way. You might still lack self-belief and wonder whether you have something valuable to bring into the room. You might be nervous about experiencing an overload of information or stimuli. You might worry that you'll annoy the director by asking 'silly' questions and slowing the process and other actors down.

Goals and obstacles

Goals
- To be able to give your best by being open and non-defensive.

Obstacles
- Lack of self-belief
- Nerves
- Tendency to become overwhelmed

- Tendency to become defensive when you feel out of your depth
- Fear of the director's opinion of you.

Strategies

1. Get your equipment together in advance

What is it?
Before you start rehearsing, the first thing you need to do is get organised with all the things you need.

Why is it useful?
Taking the time to get organised will make you feel in control, energised and ready.

How do I do it?
Go to a stationery shop (or your own cupboard if you've got a big stash of stuff already) and get yourself:

- A notebook
- A pen
- A pencil
- Highlighters
- Coloured paper to make notes on, if you find colours helpful
- Overlays to change the colour of the paper to suit you
- A folder which you can place everything in, or your tablet/laptop if you work best with screens.

Also make sure you've got together all the work you did on your script when you were researching, analysing and working on the lines.

Now you're ready to start work with the rest of the cast and creative team!

2. Ask for what you need

What is it?
Asking clearly and simply for the small adjustments, clarifications and reminders that will help you do your best work in the room.

Why is it useful?
You may be in a habit of struggling along and not letting on when you are confused, or falling a bit behind. No one can help you if you don't let them know what you need, so asking politely will empower you, and help your director and others in the team to support you too.

How do I do it?
The key question you might be asking yourself is:

> 'Should I tell them I'm dyslexic?'

The answer is yes! As long as you can also tell them how you like to work. Then you are not presenting them with a problem, or an excuse, you're filling them in with useful information that will help them to get the best work out of you.

For example:

> 'Repetition is essential.'

> 'I'd love you to model what you'd like from me so that I can see it really clearly.'

'I learn best if I'm taking in one or two instructions at a time and digesting them fully before you give me more.'

'I'll respond best if you phrase things with motivation.'

Tell the director, stage manager and the rest of the cast what to expect of you in the space, which might be:
- Slower processing
- Inability to put thoughts clearly into words
- Genius and magic!

And let them know what they can do to help you, whether that's reprinting the script on coloured paper, taking more regular five-minute breaks, or anything else. They're there to work with you, not against you.

When the director asks you questions, and you have no idea what is going on, don't clam up or be defensive or rude. It's ok to say...
- 'Can you remind me...'
- 'Let me think...'
- 'Can we recap from just before...?'
- 'Can we go back a bit?'

3. Consider your rehearsal room attitude/persona

What is it?
Maintaining a positive sense of self in the rehearsal room, and being a pleasure to work with.

Why is it useful?
It will boost your own confidence, and make others want to employ or work with you again!

How do I do it?
Take ownership – How you learn best, and how you keep up, is for YOU to work out and OWN. The way you learn is your challenge, it's not the challenge of the director or anyone else around you. Decide in advance how best to capture the information the director is giving you, so you know what you're doing. You need to feel relaxed with your process. It is important to share your process too, so others know how best to work with you.

Radiate, don't drain – Be aware if you have a tendency to withdraw into yourself – it can seem unfriendly and isolating. You have your own unique spirit in the space. You have a place in the team, and you bring an energy which will have an impact on those around you. Never be defensive, and only share your curiosities, questions and queries positively.

Accept, support and encourage – The main rule of improvisation is always to accept the offerings of your fellow actors. Keep this maxim in mind when others are making suggestions generally in a rehearsal room. Accept contributions.

Play! – Find your joy, spirit and your inner child. Be uninhibited and intrigued. The team around you will respect this and respond accordingly.

Be different and quirky – Not all communication needs to be academic or spoken in eloquent language. If you're intimated by other people's skill at expressing themselves, don't be. Use feelings, atmospheres, sensations, colour, materials and more – think outside the box and make different offerings. Others will enjoy this about you, and learn from it too.

Smile! – A confused grumpy face is a trial for anyone, particularly a director who has to sit at the front and look at you all day long. If you don't understand and need clarification, ask. Once you understand, they will be happy. It is their job to enable you to understand – and your job to try.

Don't put yourself down! – Comments like *'Sorry, you know what I'm like, I never get it right'* bring you down and also the people you're sharing it with. It's uncomfortable and unprofessional. Be eager to try again and to try differently. Be solution-focused.

Have confidence – In particular, remember that a director writing notes is not always writing about YOU!

If you feel overwhelmed at any point, take a minute to breathe deeply. There are instructions for 'a mindful minute' on page 239.

4. Capture, accept and absorb your director's notes

What is it?
Over the course of the rehearsal process, and particularly once you get into runs and early performances, your

director will give you notes on your performance. There is a knack to taking these notes on board.

Why is it useful?
Just like a visually challenged person might bring a dog, you should bring your own resources of choice to support you in capturing the director's notes. This will increase their confidence in you and your confidence in yourself.

How do I do it?
Firstly, think about how you receive the note in the moment when it's given to you verbally.

Feedback isn't criticism – it's the offering of solutions to overall problems. Do not stare blankly at the director when they give notes. It is hard for them to know what you are thinking from a blank face. Give the director a nod, a smile and let them see you capture the information.

To do this, consider:
- A reduced-sized A5 script for your back pocket, with a pen.
- Printing different acts on different coloured paper.
- Post-it notes, with tricky lines or scenes on, that fit into your pocket.
- Verbally echoing back to the director what has been agreed, as you understand it.
- A recording app on your device which allows you to capture what is said in the rehearsal room, to process later.

Share with your stage management team and director the resources you'll be using to enable yourself.

Some dos and don'ts for receiving notes:

Don'ts
- Don't dwell on the note 'personally'. Accept it as helpful on a practical level, and move on.
- Don't tell the director why you did what you did. It wastes time, and the director is asking you to change it now.
- Don't sulk – you won't get work again.
- It's not wrong to disagree or to question others' views, but don't shut others down and exclude their ideas.
- Don't be aggressive or rude, or only 'appear' to accept things and plan to ignore them.
- Don't withdraw if you're lost.

Dos
- If you don't understand the note – say so.
- Remember – the director does not favour the celeb in the cast, or other actors, over you.
- Give them praise when you think it's a good or useful note! Directors are as scared as you inside.

Wellbeing

As a dyslexic person you have *everything* you need to be an actor.

You can play, react, listen, imagine, empathise, transform. You can be intuitive, emotionally available, active, engaged, energetic, committed, determined. You break rules to fit your logic, you're a big picture thinker, spontaneous, courageous, you have a desire for fairness and truth, you can build relationships and understand humanity. So I assure you, (if you can get the finances to tally, but more on that from page 272!) you're very suited to this career.

From the exploration you did in Part One into your identity, you will now have a sense of who you are as a dyslexic individual. This is a solid foundation to move forward from.

However, coping with the industry can be very difficult.

Goals and obstacles

Goal
To cope with life in this crazy industry.

Obstacles
As you now know, dyslexic people respond best to:
- Structure
- Routine
- Safety
- Openness
- Simplicity
- Clarity
- Empowerment.

The acting profession doesn't always meet these needs. It demands you move out of this structured comfort zone.

Sometimes when you're working there is a clear routine, e.g. rehearsals 10-6 p.m., or a show in the evening.

Sometimes you'll have no acting work for weeks and your time is yours to do what you want with.

Often you'll get an audition through and need to suddenly drop everything to prep for two days. Agents ask for spontaneity. There are cancellations, alterations, time changes, venue moves and often little feedback. In addition you'll most probably have 'another job' to pay the bills alongside acting and so you'll need to manage your time well – time is money, and you will need to have excellent time management skills.

You also need *resilience*. (An ability to bounce back). To have resilience you need to be able to monitor your wellbeing. Being emotionally available is essential when acting, but it can be painful digging deep inside and unearthing past experiences. Other people would only ever do this in a safe space with a professional expert. As an actor you don't have a professional supporting you and your mental health.

Paradoxically you also need to be tough to cope with rejection. For most of the auditions you do, you will not be a complete fit. That's normal. You need to be able to accept it wasn't something you did wrong. Once the audition is over you have to find a way to forget it and move on. This is hard! (But you can read some strategies for this on page 216.)

It's no surprise in the acting industry that drugs and alcohol addictions are common. They ease feelings and numb what's really going on inside. They work momentarily to block pain and hide the truth. Isolation, loneliness and anxiety set in and, of course, it all starts to control you. This can, of course, be exacerbated if you are dyslexic and have low self-esteem.

The acting industry is a tough one. This chapter will offer some tools to cope with it.

Strategies

A 2023 Harvard study said that one in every two people in the world will develop a mental health disorder in their lifetime.

To be an actor you need to be a 'well being'.

Like your craft, your health is psycho-physical, involving the mind and body. Mental and physical health go hand in hand.

These strategies will help you establish healthy life practices to improve your wellbeing and help you find calm, contentment and proactivity.

Work through them systematically, and remember, it takes time and commitment to change habits.

1. Life pie

What is it?
In this strategy you create a life pie chart to take a bird's eye look at all the different areas of your life and how content you are with these areas.

Why is it useful?
It is important to make time for your friends and family as well as working hard and keeping fit. Finding a good balance in these different areas helps keep your mind healthy and happy. The life pie lays out aspects of your life visually so you can ponder making changes to rebalance your wellbeing.

How do I do it?
Copy the big circle below. Label each slice of the pie with the different areas of your life. These areas might be:
- Finances
- Family
- Partner
- Friendships
- Career
- Mental health
- Fitness
- Hobbies

Now shade in each area with a coloured pencil according to how satisfied you are with the area. Fully shaded means you're very satisfied, not shaded at all means very unsatisfied.

Have a look at the model below to help.

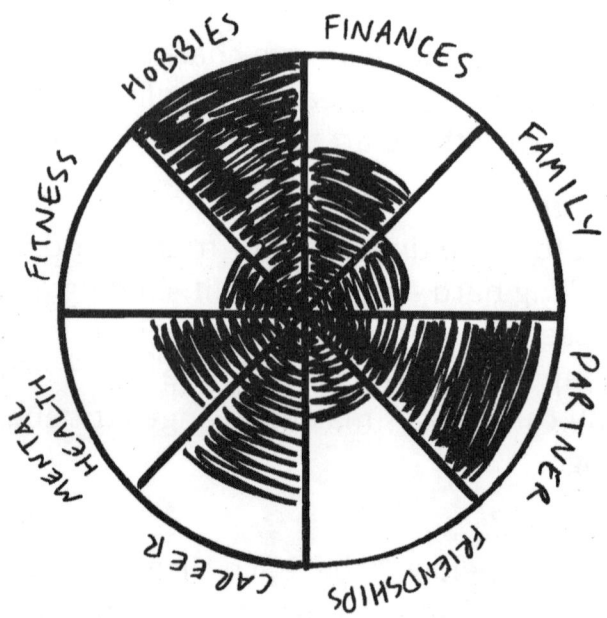

The less shaded areas show you where you need to invest a bit more time and effort.

What does this tell you? Are there any areas that need altering? Changes can occur when we think and reflect. If you plan to make changes, will it improve your wellbeing? How will you go about altering these aspects of your life?

Now have a go...

Part Three: Your Career

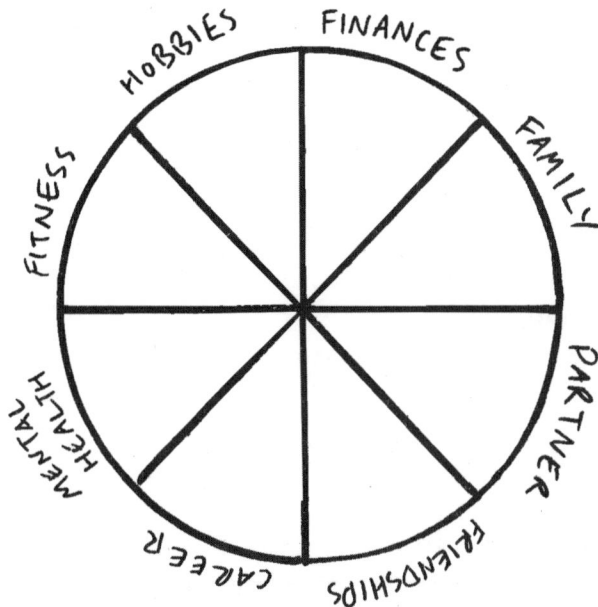

What do you notice?

2. Wellbeing pie of positive habits

What is it?
This pie chart examines your attitude to life, to your self and to others.

Why is it useful?
Often, we're not aware of the little habits we have that bring our mood and ourselves down. By examining how many of these negative mindset habits you have, you become more aware of what you're doing to inhibit your own wellbeing. You can then make a concerted effort to enforce the positive habits that you're not doing. This should set you on the path to become a happier and more fulfilled version of yourself.

How do I do it?
Go to the big circle below. Label each slice of the pie with a different positivity habit. These habits are:
- Finding things to be grateful for/positive about
- Speaking with honesty
- Not putting yourself down to others
- Not gossiping about others
- Using kind words
- Looking for the good in things
- Appreciating the small and natural things around you
- Getting rid of the negative 'imposter' talking to you in your head.

Take some time to shade in the diagram according to how satisfied you are with these different areas.

If you do this pie twice a year and keep them, you will notice valuable insights.

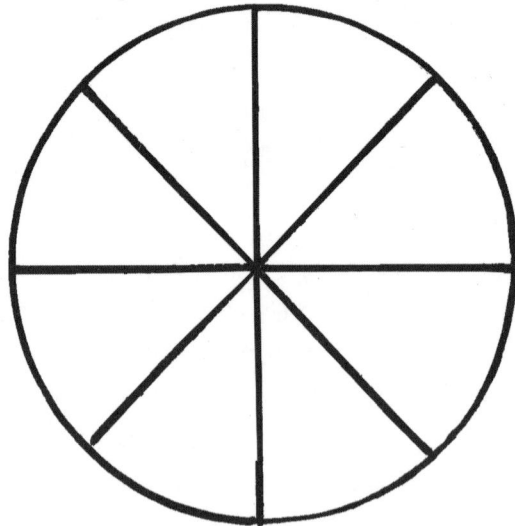

Write at the bottom what you notice.

Part Three: Your Career

3. Banishing the devil of doubt

What is it?
We often have a little devil lurking inside us putting us down. We need to kick it out!

It's brought on by the fact that you can't truly see yourself from the outside.
You don't see what others see: your achievements, your amazing personality, your creativity and drive.

Instead you allow this 'imposter' into the equation to stir up negative thoughts.
Don't. It destroys your wellbeing and robs you of who you REALLY are. For wellbeing you are only interested in the FACTS.

Why is it useful?
Positive re-enforcement is vital for being well.

How do I do it?
Go back to the resources you created in the chapter on Identity and revisit your strengths. You'll find them in your Jelly Person from Strategy 3 (page 22). A part of staying well is continually remembering these.

In this strategy, simply add to that existing list nice things people have said to you – yes compliments!

And read it, often!

4. Positive actions

What is it?
A list of actions you can carry out that will keep you feeling well.

Why is it useful?
The power of positivity is unbelievable, and it works!

How do I do it?

- Mix with people who radiate positive energy
- Try to find a positive way around difficulties by using your problem-solving skills
- Listen more than you talk
- Keep active – breathe
- Apologise when you get things wrong
- Stay in touch with friends and family
- Celebrate
- Play (music, sing, dance, jump, skip, run)
- Tell people you love them (if you do!)
- Ask for help
- Find times to be mindful, present in the moment
- Smile and laugh
- Carry out random acts of kindness
- Act on your ideas and instigate new projects
- Visualise your future with a positive goal.

From time to time it is just good practice to check in with our thinking and how we operate day to day.

5. Action equals 'doing', not just thinking

What is it?
So much of your acting career requires self-motivation to actually do things. To *find* work, *make* work, *practise* work, and be proactive. This best occurs when you are feeling positive and motivated, and actually 'doing' something.

Start each day with an action, a thing to do, a goal to achieve, however small.

Why is it useful?
Doing things keeps us well. Talking about doing things does not! Turning thoughts into action is a guaranteed winner.

How do I do it?
Every person will find different methods of surging into action effectively – from drinking a cup of coffee, to listening to a podcast by a great actor. It takes practice and a lot of self-observation to find out what motivates you.

Start noticing and noting down *when* you feel positive and motivated.

Is it:
- A good call with your agent?
- Coming up with an amazing idea for a piece at a theatre festival?
- A motivating get-together with other creatives or actor friends?
- An acting workshop?

- After reading through your strengths and achievements and CV?
- Doing research and development?

Once you know what boosts your mood into action, note the process down and do it!

6. Accountability buddies

What is it?
We all need to be accountable and take responsibility for completing the tasks we set out to achieve. Very few people are good at doing this alone. We move goal posts and procrastinate. Find a buddy to meet each month and set yourselves three simple goals to work towards.

Why is it useful?
Having someone to motivate you really helps. 'A problem shared is a problem halved'. They can support you in a mutually safe space from an 'outside yourself' perspective. Best of all, it works for them too. As you know, a dyslexic loves collaboration and problem-solving.

How do I do it?
With your 'buddy', pick a date each month to meet up. Choose the date, stick to it and make it matter. When you are flaky or postpone, it makes it appear unimportant.

When you meet up, keep it simple:
- Set a timer for 5/10 minutes.
- The first person speaks, with the other listening.
- Start by discussing what is holding you back and what you're finding challenging.

- At the end of 5 minutes the listener asks 'open' questions, for example:
  o 'What skills do you have that could support you in improving this situation?
  o 'What one action could you take to move forward?'
  o 'What do you think is the one big thing holding you back?'
- Allow person one to reflect slowly.
- After this, give them time to set three goals that feel comfortable and possible to achieve in the next month, in order to improve on this situation.
- Swap over to person two.

If it's helpful, check in each week with each other by text or phone. Meet a month later to reflect on the findings. What has worked? What didn't work? What have you learned from this? What might you try differently next time?

Never underestimate the use of this accountability buddy. It does take discipline but is well worth it.

> **Buddy tips**
> Questions are far more important than advice and statements, or 'if I were you' – you are not them and they must decide their way. What is challenging for them may not be for you, and vice versa – your role is to allow them space to find the answers for themselves.

7. Mindfulness

What is it?
I've never known a word confuse so many dyslexic people as 'mindfulness'. I like to think of mindfulness as a technique to calm and comfort a 'mind full of mess'.

Why is it useful?
A mind that is often overwhelmed with exciting creative ideas, and working twice as much as most individuals to keep up, deserves a break. It needs calm and comfort to improve wellbeing.

Taking a minute for some mindfulness meditation or breathing, can do wonders to get you back on track.

You are operating in a highly competitive profession with ever changing schedules. Mindfulness can stop you reacting foolishly, jumping to wrong conclusions, and allowing your emotions to take over.

When you're pumped full of adrenaline and about to blow up, mindful breathing works. You can never control what happens to you, but you can always control how you deal with it.

How do I do it?
There are plenty of apps which guide you through regular mindful meditation, so search the app store on your device to see what's available.

If you don't want to use an app, or if you just want a go now, here's a simple meditation for you to try:

A mindful minute
- Take a slow deep breath in
- Slowly fill your lungs to capacity
- Close your eyes and relax
- Hold your breath for 3 seconds
- Enjoy the calmness
- Breathe out fully
- Take another slow deep breath in
- Hold this breath for 3 seconds
- Breathe out fully
- As you breathe out, relax your jaw and shoulders
- Concentrate on one breath at a time
- Nothing else
- If your thoughts wander off, simply notice your breathing again
- A repeated mindful minute of breathing can keep you well for the day.

When should I use mindfulness?
It's good to get in the habit of practising mindfulness regularly. Try inserting 10 minutes each morning into your daily routine. This will leave you generally feeling calmer and more able to cope. You can also use mindfulness if you suddenly find yourself feeling stressed and emotionally overloaded.

For example:
An email bugs you. Just before you explode and have a tantrum, close the machine.

Take a mindful minute going through the exercise above.

When you return to the email, ask yourself:

> 'What is going on here that is bugging me so much? Was the tone bossy? Am I feeling that it's unfair?'

Now ask:

> 'What are the FACTS? Is there a different way of looking at this?'

8. Yoga

What is it?
Yoga is a physical, mental, and spiritual practice originating in ancient India. It is holistic, which means it works both the mind and the body – perfect for actors' wellbeing!

Why is it useful?
Your body is your actor's tool. Your body needs to be supple and strong. Being able to perform without holding tension is vital, and that includes natural breathing. Each thought an actor speaks comes from breath, and we tend to hold our breath when we're nervous. Train yourself to keep your breath flowing like a river and you will feel free. It will enable you to react freely and spontaneously.

Yoga offers a practice that helps you do this. It frees tension and encourages focus through connecting the mind with the body. Plus, it develops increased flexibility, muscle strength and tone. Add this into your weekly wellbeing programme and you will never be sorry.

How do I do it?
If you're a yoga novice it's really best to start in the room with a teacher as it's important to make sure your alignment is correct and that you are doing positions correctly and safely. If not you can become injured. Although yoga classes are often expensive, studios often offer discount trial rates. Once you have a basic grasp of the postures, there are lots of classes online, and videos you can follow in your own time on YouTube.

9. Therapy/counselling and mentoring

What is it?
There are many types of therapy involving different methodologies that aim for better wellbeing. They help you deal with difficulties you're facing. They're principally based on you talking to another human being about yourself in a safe space. An opportunity to share behavioural patterns, relationships to people, how you feel and why.

Why is it useful?
Therapy can help you work through issues that have been building for a long time and give you the tools to address difficulties instead of burying them. Issues we bury always come and bite us in the end, and it's so valuable to learn 'how' to deal properly with difficulties.

How do I do it?
Visit your GP to ask, or find a practitioner privately. It is an expensive process, but when you are established, nothing is more replenishing than dealing with issues that

are blocking your wellbeing and creativity. Don't suffer in silence. Ask for support.

Some therapy resources to try
The Minster Centre in London trains people in psychotherapy and counselling, but also offers affordable therapy, staffed by students of that training: **minstercentre.ac.uk**

The Samaritans offer a confidential listening service on the phone, 24 hours a day, if you call 116 123 from any phone. They also list specialist organisations to help you more specifically, on this webpage: **samaritans.org/how-we-can-help/if-youre-having-difficult-time/other-sources-help**

SANEline is a national out-of-hours mental health helpline offering specialist emotional support, guidance and information to anyone affected by mental illness, including family, friends and carers. They are normally open every day of the year from 4 p.m. to 10 p.m. on 0300 304 7000: **sane.org.uk/what_we_do/support/helpline**

The British Association for Behavioural and Cognitive Psychotherapies is the lead organisation for Cognitive Behavioural Therapy (CBT) in the UK and Ireland. Their website offers a list of accredited therapists: **babcp.com/CBTRegister**

The Counselling Directory is what its name suggests, a searchable directory of in-person and online counsellors, by location: **counselling-directory.org.uk**

NHS Talking Therapies, for anxiety and depression, is a programme of NHS-based talking therapy support – for which you can be referred, or you can refer yourself. You can read more about it at **www.england.nhs.uk/mental-health/adults/nhs-talking-therapies**

Mind is a charity whose aim is to bring awareness about mental health to the fore, and to offer information and advice. They have an info line through which you can ask about mental health problems, where to get help near you, treatment options, advocacy services, and welfare benefits. Call 0300 123 3393 or visit **mind.org.uk**

If you are a member of Equity, the performing arts and entertainment trade union, you can access information and help with mental health issues through them too. Go to **equity.org.uk/advice-and-support/dignity-at-work/mental-health-support**

> Go to this book's web page: **www.nickhernbooks.co.uk/dat-resources** to find all these links available for you to click through.

10. Eat healthily

What is it?
Your brain uses more energy than any other organ in your body. It needs a continuous stream of energy, even when sleeping. During my time working in this field, I have certainly noticed that mood disorders like depression and

chronic anxiety can be made worse simply by fluctuating blood sugar levels. This also affects memory, attention and language (cognitive function), something inadvisable for most people, let alone dyslexic actors!

Why is it useful?
We are what we eat! Eating a healthier, more balanced diet will lift your mood, give you more energy over a longer sustained period of time and also prevent many poor diet-related illnesses.

How do I do it?
Here's a rough guide to food that's good to eat when you just can't make a decision. Aim to feed your dyslexic brain and eat something regularly, every 4 hours when in demanding mental situations. For example, a regular nutritious portion at 8 a.m., 12 noon, 4 p.m., and 7 p.m.

Enjoy:
- Fruit
- Veggies – a good source of vitamins and minerals, including Vitamins B, C and potassium
- Raw juices – bursting with vital nutrients
- Nuts and seeds – containing protein, healthy fats, fibres, vitamins, and minerals
- Whole grains, which provide fibre, vitamins, minerals and other nutrients
- Good quality proteins such as lean meat, poultry, fish, beans and lentils.

Avoid:
- White bread
- Fizzy drinks
- Sugar
- White pasta
- Alcohol*
- Caffeine.

* Yes, some of us love it, but be mindful that alcohol is a depressant.

11. Exercise

What is it?
We all know what exercise is, but what we need is a form of activity that raises your heart rate. It makes you stronger, fitter and more able to cope with the physical demands of the acting profession.

Why is it useful?
Exercise helps you really breathe. It supports you to become the authentic you; happier, stronger and sharper. Raising your heart rate burns calories, and intervals of gentle followed by higher impact exercise give amazing results. Add this into your wellbeing programme.

How do I do it?
You don't have to have a costly gym membership. Twenty minutes to an hour of regular cardio exercise develops fitness and wellbeing. Do it three times a week. It opens you up to being responsive to the world. Walk, jog, cycle with your phone turned off and notice what's around you.

12. Create your mantra

What is it?
You are, or want to be, a fulfilled successful actor. How you see success is up to you. One thing is certain – only *you* can set your mind to achieve this. A mantra to chant, a mantra to remind you of your goal, in that moment, can be a great way of motivating yourself.

Why is it useful?
'Mantra' is a term derived from two Sanskrit words: 'manas' meaning 'mind' and 'tra' meaning 'tool'. Speaking words aloud, and hearing these words and 'meaning' these words, is a very powerful motivational tool for the mind. It releases stress, creates motivation and reaffirms goals.

How do I do it?
Take a short phrase and repeat it to yourself as a chant, as you are doing your exercise, yoga, or just walking along.

The mantra can be as simple as – 'I am ready for this audition challenge', or 'I have everything needed to smash this'.

It is best of all if you follow a process to create an appropriate mantra based on true positive experience, so that know as you repeat it to yourself that it is rooted in facts:

Make a list of your top three achievements in your career so far.

Then write down how you managed to achieve them.

Finally, combine these ideas to find out what the *belief* was that made you act in a certain way and led to your achievements.

Here is an example:

What I achieved: I got a role I was really excited to play.

How I made it happen: I built a great relationship with the director in a previous project, and I kept an eye out for projects that they were going to work on in future, then I made contact directly to put myself forward.

Why I did it: I want to advance my career and to work with people who value my work.

My underlying belief: I have the ability to make things happen for myself by being proactive and a pleasure to work with.

Your mantra might be 'I have the focus and determination to make things happen for myself' or 'I am somebody people want to work with again and again', or 'I am a proactive self-starter.'

13. Inspiration gallery

What is it?
A collection of visual images – photos and pictures – that inspire and motivate you.

Why is it useful?
An inspiration gallery is a fantastic visual flash reminder of what it's possible to achieve. It can help keep you focused on making what you want happen for you.

How do I do it?
Print and cut out pictures of people that you admire; those who you want to make work with; those who you want to take advice from; and roles they have played.

What they have done is possible, you can achieve this too!

Stick them onto your wall separately or create a giant collage, somewhere where you'll regularly see it – in your bedroom, or by your desk – to act as a reminder of what you're aspiring to.

Time management and organisation

Along with the importance of staying well, living as a dyslexic person means learning how to manage your time effectively.

Time is everything. As a living, breathing, vibrant being it's your most precious asset. It's something you need to understand the concept of, respect and honour. There's no option of being late for a meeting, rehearsal or performance. Unless it's a 'one-off, rarely happens' occasion, it can harm your reputation, career and wellbeing.

I have noticed that the two 'sides' to a dyslexic identity can create a real conundrum when it comes to time management:

1. When you have an idea, your curiosity is captured, you're intrigued and you want to achieve that goal. You are off. Your belief system can see no barriers, determination kicks in, energy fills your mind and body, and action takes place. Force and drive take over, propelling you forward, enabling you to achieve anything, find all the necessary resilience and become unstoppable.

2. But what happens when the other part of your identity kicks in? You notice you start to forget things, you become disorientated, you can't connect to the task. Tiredness hits your brain and body; even the smallest decision can't be made. You can't remember what you've read, what was agreed. You start to question your ability, cover up the stress and worry, and you collapse. It's disorientating when you wonder which part of your character you will hit on what day.

(Let me add that every human can have this, but it is more exaggerated in a dyslexic person).

To function well as an actor, you don't want to see-saw between productively using time and wasting it. This causes a lot of mental strain and uses huge amounts of energy. You need to create a balanced and predictable time-regime that you can rely upon.

Managing time and having things in order makes all of life easier. It is empowering and healthy. With a structured process and routine in place, organisation becomes a part of your day, and the swinging up and down of your effectiveness steadies out. You need to put strategies in place to balance your surging ups and downs.

Time is money, organisation is reputation, reputation gives you repeated work and income. All this brings satisfaction and raises self-esteem.

So in order to move forward you need to understand time. How many days, hours, minutes it takes to DO things. How many days, hours, minutes do you have before a deadline?

The concept of how long five minutes actually is, and what can be achieved in those five minutes, can be surprising. You may notice the voice in your head saying, 'take a shower, pack your bag and leave ASAP!' but a lack of focus and an ability to be distracted leads you off on another path. You put washing on and feed the cat, then you can't find your shoes or keys, and you leave late having gone round and round in circles. Chasing your tail day after day is not good! Dithering and faffing and fussing about what to do first, means you're actually not doing anything. This creates mind mess.

So, if you're now thinking, 'That's me! That's what I do. But *how* do I change ...?', work through the strategies below. Yes, they take time, but in the long run they will save you so much more time and help you work in a focused and consistent way. You'll be very happy you invested the time.

> ## Goals and obstacles
> **Goal**
> - To be efficient and organised.
>
> **Obstacles**
> - Having a skewed perception of how long things take
> - Being messy and chaotic
> - Lacking focus
> - Not being able to see the bigger picture of your commitments and responsibilities
> - Finding it difficult to plan ahead.

Strategies

These strategies are designed to give you what you need to achieve: mindset, discipline and purpose.

1. Relationship with time

What is it?
This strategy helps you work out how long it actually takes you to complete a certain task, compared with how long you think it takes you. So you can more accurately plan your days and work.

Why is it useful?
Learning how long it actually takes you to accomplish

tasks means you can plan precisely and avoid the added stress of rushing. Knowing how long to spend on each task, and making sure that each tiny part of the job doesn't lead to *another* full-blown activity, is a talent and worth practising!

How do I do it?
Write down a list of tasks you do every day.

For example:
- Taking a shower and dressing
- Having breakfast
- Getting up and leaving the house, from start to finish
- Door-to-door commute
- Walking to the nearest transport from home
- Doing your daily or weekly shopping.

Now guess how long it takes you to accomplish each of these tasks. Write it next to the task.

Over the next week, time yourself doing all of these activities.

How long does it *actually* take you?

Write the actual time next to the guessed time.

What's the difference between the two?

Have you not been leaving enough time for yourself, and getting stressed instead? Had you been allowing way too much time, and wasting days? Are you good at judging accurately?

2. Organising your calendar/diary

What is it?
Keeping an organised diary is key to managing your time effectively. This strategy will lay out a few different forms of calendars/diaries with tips. Have a go at all of them and see which one works best for you.

Why is it useful?
It means you don't have to keep every appointment and task in your head – so you're less likely to forget any, but also, you can check your availability carefully before you agree to things: Don't just say 'yes', 'yes', 'yes', and live with the mess it creates.

How do I do it?
Work out what kind of diary you like best. A virtual phone diary or a paper, physical copy to write in and touch.

Phone diary apps
If you respond best to having a diary on your phone, you can either use your phone's calendar or download an independent app. Both your phone's in-built calendar function and any app you choose to download will allow you to decide on a colour code for different areas of your work, for example:
- Pink for work
- Blue for social
- Green for exercise
- Red for prep.

You can also use these apps to set reminders.

Physical diaries

There are lots of different diaries with different layouts. You might try, for example, a diary with the week on one side, and lines for notes on the other. Divide the notes page into seven, in keeping with the lines separating the days on the left-hand side. Then write deadlines and meetings on the left-hand side, and on the right, the prep you need to do for those deadlines and meetings.

Don't let yourself become overwhelmed. Remember that every single thing you do in a day takes time, and this time needs to be factored into your calendar in order for it to get done.

> **When adding items to your diary, remember:**
>
> Every appointment you say yes to:
> - Has a travel time to get *to* it
> - Needs preparation time *before* it
> - And it has a *use* to you.
>
> Before you say yes, think of these three things.
> - How long is the travel time? This must be marked out in your diary
> - What must I prepare beforehand? You must factor this time into your diary entry too
> - And finally, is it useful to me (or am I doing a favour?).
>
> As you do this task you analyse your time realistically and structure a good time practice.

3. Offloading

What is it?
We all know what it's like: more and more people are making demands on your time, and the longer it goes on, the worse it gets. You can't think how or where to begin with all that needs to be done. You're burying your head in the sand and soon to come crashing down…

To offload all that needs to be done, you're going to get it all into your calendar as an element of time.

Why is it useful?
Taking everything out of your head and putting it on paper immediately calms you. It tidies up the mess in your head. You can clearly see what to do and how to achieve it, laid out for you in easy-to-follow steps. When the offload is done, the *action* starts.

How do I do it?

> **Note:** The instructions here are for a physical process of offloading with pen and paper, but there are apps available that will help you to do the same thing – you can research them online.

Write headings at the top of three separate pages: 'Home', 'Work' and 'Social'.

Now, write down everything you need to do, in no particular order, in three long lists under these headings.

Now think about how long it's going to take you to achieve each task. Write the length of time next to the task.

Open your diary. Look at your week/s ahead.

First of all, add in the space and time for other activities that you know form part of your daily routine. The ones that aren't on your offload list – like going to your regular yoga class.

Now consider your offload list. Which task fits where? Offload the task into your calendar, allocating each task with a specific time and day.

> **Remember** to be realistic with your time, and add in travel!
>
> It takes discipline and determination to understand time and be firm with it. If you are marking your activities with a realistic number of minutes or hours, this will work.
>
> If you run out of time for the activity on one day, remember to leave more minutes for the next time you do this task, and rearrange the next day's activities.
>
> If you have extra time (or arrive to appointments early) great! You can prepare.

4. Longer-term planner

What is it?
The big-picture planner gives you an idea of what's ahead.

When your career is up and down it focuses you on how to begin a project, breaking it into smaller, manageable chunks. There are many different ways in which to do this, and with time and practice you will find yours.

Why is it useful?
Taking the time to plan out the weeks or months ahead for a new job or project will calm and relax you. You'll be able to look forward, feeling confident that you're prepared and ready to go.

How do I do it?
Let's say you have a role in a play, and you want to organise your time correctly to have everything in shape.

Julie Andrews sang 'let's start at the very beginning', but you are dyslexic, so I suggest you start at the end and work backwards!

1. Buy or print a year or month-to-view planner, and shade in what you know is fact: the performing dates.
2. Mark in the rehearsal period that falls before the performances. With or without a detailed schedule you will have the overall rehearsal dates as soon as you're offered the job.
3. Shade in private preparation time before rehearsals start for your own individual process of research and learning.

When marking time for learning, remember that short chunks of focused learning work best, repeated and interspersed with other small tasks.

> **Alternative approaches**
>
> **Create your own timeline**
> If the kinds of long-term planners you can buy freak you out or are too busy for you, make your own with a big roll of paper that you can stick on your wall.
>
> **Use colour or images**
> Put different months on your planner in different colours, or use different colours for different projects, or for different parts of the process (e.g. personal preparation in blue, rehearsals in pink and shooting or performances in orange).
>
> Some of us don't process words so well, and images work better, so play with laying out the tasks you need to accomplish with pictures – you can print, draw, collage, whatever you fancy!

5. Filing

What is it?
Keeping important documents safe! We all have those scary piles of important papers that we don't want to think about. This strategy sets out a quick and simple way of sorting all these administrative bits of paper.

Part Three: Your Career

This strategy can also be transferred to your computer – if you don't receive letters or bank statements on paper, and you don't tend to print off audition scripts, or contracts, for example, you will still have those things in your emails or in documents saved in your computer. Perhaps they're all in one huge unsorted list in your 'Downloads' folder...

Why is it useful?
Firstly it shows you how much better it feels to have attempted and achieved something. Then on top of that you're saving yourself a lot of time and stress when you need to find a document.

How do I do it?
1. Buy six folders of different colours and/or create six folders on your computer (ideally, these folders would be saved in the Cloud as well, so that you can access them from other devices or while you are out and about – look into cloud storage options for this). For physical folders I prefer box files to ring-binders as it means you don't have to spend time hole-punching.
Label each folder. For example:
1 – Acting work (contracts, CV, scripts...)
2 – Non-acting work (contracts, payslips...)
3 – Banking and finance (current accounts, savings accounts, loans, credit cards...)
4 – Tax (receipts, print-outs of tax returns, communications with accountant...)
5 – Home (utility bills, council tax demands, rent or mortgage documents, parking permits...)

  6 – Valuables (certificates, passport, MOT certificates and car logbook...)
2. Now get hold of that pile of paperwork we mentioned (or that great long Downloads folder). Set thirty minutes on your alarm. Go through each item and put it into one of the folders. Decide quickly and simply, don't overthink – just get through it. It's only thirty minutes of your full attention and focus. No phone distraction.
3. When the thirty minutes is up, have a break. Grab a drink and reflect on how that went. Do you have more to go through still? Set yourself another thirty minutes.

Faffing gets nothing done. Find the drive and determination to focus on the result, and apply it to the task. (When you're in the movie, you can pay someone else to do it!)

Done it all but raring for more?!

Separate each folder into smaller categories.
For example, your Home folder could be divided into:

- Electricity
- Gas
- Water
- Council tax
- Rent/mortgage.

Now having done the task, reflect. Ask yourself: 'what have I achieved?' Do I like having more categories, and do I have the time to file this deeply, moving forward? The secret is not to over-focus and read through all the documents in detail, but to keep the mindset 'I'm filing these quickly.'

> **Remember** it might not be necessary to keep everything. Do you need that water bill from eight years ago? Perhaps 'Folder 7' should be THE BIN.

6. The Command Centre

What is it?
In this strategy you locate an area in your room or house that you devote solely to important things and life admin – without having to move it. The fruit bowl is not recommended!

Why is it useful?
There's a definite visual plus to having one allocated place where all important things live. Visually noting what you have in front of you, and knowing where valuables live, saves time. It also means you're far less likely to keep misplacing important items if you know they are meant to be *here*.

How do I do it?
Find a flat surface and make it a hallowed space – the Command Centre! Whenever you aren't using them, put your wallet, travelcard, keys, diary, phone and laptop or tablet on the flat space. Ideally, you'd also keep your open diary there – with the current week visible over two pages.

You could use a kitchen cupboard with a worktop beneath. Maybe attach hooks to the inside door of the cupboard, so you can hang keys to different things. Keep your important documents/filing boxes on the shelf. Have pens, envelopes, etc. handy there too. Keep your laptop on the work surface, with lists and on-going project work next to it.

When valuable things have a specific 'place' it is easy to notice when something is missing.

When you come home, don't just dump your things around your room. Make a routine of getting to the Command Centre first. And do not let anyone else touch or move the items in this space!

7. Distraction alert – the phone!

What is it?
In order to stay sane, you need to keep on top of texts and emails. But you must NOT be a slave to your phone. Messages are sent 24/7 to you because the working day has now extended to any time, any place. You live in a world where 'instant' is a way of life. That's why keeping well is so hard to do because of the pressure all around.

Mistakes are made by looking at messages quickly, and not doing the back-up work. This exercise equips you with strategies to put in place to stop you from doing this. Being a slave to your phone will *not* keep you well.

Why is it useful?
Looking at information continually throughout the day:
- Distracts
- Adds to anxiety
- Is unnecessary
- Takes, and wastes, your time.

How do I do it?

> **Note:** Naturally, if your phone actually *rings* at any time, you should pick it up. This strategy is for dealing with the times when you're tempted to pick it up and *check* it, unprompted.

One approach to try is only to look at your phone at lunchtime and once in the evening – when you are able to reflect with your calendar on your availability. But when looking at other apps, distractions flash through. You will have to be strong.

Being out of contact can actually be empowering, and enable you to be in control of your pressure-load and to embrace what is around you more fully.

- Carry out an experiment. For a couple of days, allow yourself to respond to messages immediately when you're contacted. How do you feel? How productive are you? How well do you feel?
- Now spend a couple of days only checking your phone in the morning and then in the evening.

What did you notice? Which did you prefer? Why?

8. The night-before prep

What is it?
It's the night before a big audition, or the start of a new project. You need to save time, sleep/rest well and not worry. By getting everything ready for the next morning you can achieve all of this!

Why is it useful?
Knowing everything is prepped and ready the day before a big event can really help calm you. It can also help you go to sleep because you've surrounded yourself with an aura of calm, mature readiness. You're good to go.

How do I do it?
1. Firstly, think through everything you'll need for tomorrow. Lunch? Your script, some pencils and highlighters? A notebook? A bottle of water? Now work systematically making sure you have everything ready.
2. Make lunch and have it in the fridge, with a fork on top, to put in your bag in the morning. The fork on top will jog your memory in the morning to put it in your bag.
3. Pack your bag. Run through what you are doing the next day chronologically, activity by activity, and put things into your bag that you need for those activities.
4. Plan your journey. Look up where you're going, how you're going to get there, and check online what the building looks like.
5. Lay out your clothes ready, to save you wasting time looking for things in the morning. Check the weather and make sure you're prepared.
6. Take a shower or a relaxing bath before bed. It soothes and nurtures.
7. Set your alarm, content that you only have to wash, clean your teeth, get dressed, eat breakfast, grab your lunch from the fridge and pick up your pre-packed bag tomorrow morning.

> **Tips for a good night's sleep**
>
> Technology interferes with your ability to go to sleep. Switch your phone to airplane mode, or leave

it in another room. Don't look at screens for at least an hour before bed.

Work out what helps lull you to sleep. Try white noise, music, meditation, reading a book. Until we experiment with what allows us to sleep, we have no way of knowing what works. The idea is to rid the brain of pointless worry – texting and watching a movie in bed only sends your mind crazy.

A warm bath or shower helps you get to sleep. It lowers your body's core temperature (which your body does before you sleep) and so mimics the body's natural cycle.

9. Time-saving warm-up  R

What is it?
Before an audition or performance you need to warm up your body and your voice and articulation. This strategy helps you work out a warm-up that you can do quickly or on-the-move, and can become a part of your regular routine.

Why is it useful?
Dyslexic individuals need familiarity, routine and structure. You can learn this short warm-up, make it your own, and do it every time. If you're pushed for time, a warm-up on the go will mean you arrive on time and ready.

How do I do it?
Here's a list of the different and necessary components that you should include in your warm-up:
- Meditation/clearing mind of mess
- Facial warm-up
- Physical warm-up
- Breath warm-up
- Lip exercises
- Tongue exercises
- Vocal warm-up.

Find one quick and quirky exercise for each component. You then have a packaged warm-up ready to go to fit these into your daily life. For example:

In the shower:
- Stand still a moment and take three deep breaths in through the nose and out through the mouth
- Massage your jaw while washing your face
- Do vocal sirening – on an 'ng' sound, slide your voice from low to high and back again
- Do horse blows with your lips, while shaking your head
- Make your face long and thin, make your face wide and fat
- Vowel shapes: exaggerate the mouth positions for 'A, E, I, O and U'.

Out of the shower:
- Spinal roll down to dry your legs and feet
- Spinal roll back up to dry your upper body

- Roll your shoulders and stretch your arms high and wide before going to get dressed.

At breakfast:
- Use exaggerated lips to take food from the spoon
- Chew your food enough times to engage your jaw.

Walking to the bus or train:
- Take whatever opportunities you can for a physical warm-up as part of your journey: take the stairs not the lift, walk up the escalator, etc.
- Tongue limbers – use your tongue to clean your teeth, all the way around, several times. Thrust your tongue out as far as you can three times
- Tongue twisters – drill your articulators with tongue-twisters (see page 41) and consonants: 'Puh-Tuh-Kuh; Buh-Duh-Guh; Wuh-Muh-Nuh'.

Sitting on the bus or train:
When you're travelling to work you can very easily whittle away the journey on your phone, doom-scrolling or texting. Why not try using that time to think about what you really want to achieve with your day, and making a note?

10. Your actor's memory book

What is it?
Your memory book is a way of keeping track of every career-related activity that happens: who you met, what was discussed, and thoughts that you had.

Why is it useful?

This notebook is many things. It's a reminder of how proactive and productive you actually are. During times when you're struggling with work or self-worth, have a look at your notebook and remind yourself that you are being active.

It's also potentially the key to future work. Each meeting, workshop, masterclass, lecture, rehearsal, and chat with an agent is a possibility for future work – so log it! You will create a memory of what happened and that's a valuable reference base.

As an actor your head must be observing and embracing the world, your mind open to all new contacts, and your enthusiasm ready to grab any opportunity that feels right. Although a meeting may not be of mutual benefit in the first instance, the following year, or when there is no work, you will have a reason to be in touch. This resource is a great investment in your career.

How do I do it?

Buy a notebook. When you meet someone or have an important call, note it down briefly in the same format each time:
- The date
- Name of the person
- Where you met
- What happened
- What was discussed – briefly
- How you felt and what you thought

- What to follow up on and when (to transfer into your diary/calendar later, when at the Command Centre!).

Write your name and contact number in the front of the book in case you leave it somewhere.

> **Note to self: Back up your files!!**
>
> If you're recording this information digitally using an app or a programme on your computer, you must remember to back the files up.
>
> Back up your phone to the Cloud.
>
> Use applications such as Dropbox or Google Docs to access the same documents on different gadgets.

General tips for time management and organisation

- Enjoy being in charge of your own time, and don't let others disrupt your planning
- Don't cancel or postpone meetings unless it's vital – it will make you feel awful
- Keep your diary and your actor's memory book (see page 269) with you at all times
- Turn your phone off when you're busy
- Detox from social media if it causes you more stress than pleasure
- Only reply to emails about appointments when your

calendar/diary is with you and you can also write anything you've agreed to down there
- If emailing is a slow process for you, keep it brief, or call people and ask them to follow up with a confirmation about what you discussed or agreed in writing
- Consider getting all the tasks, activities and deadlines in your head that are making you anxious down in mind map or diagram form, or a list
- Identify times and places where you work and focus best
- Always finish with reflection, i.e. thinking about how you've learned from your experiences: What worked? What didn't? What strategies should you keep, and which ones should you scrap?

Living as a dyslexic actor can be the most rewarding and fulfilling lifestyle if you are able to find the balance needed to function well.

Finances

There cannot be an actor in the world who finds the finance side of life bearable! It's no secret that working in the arts can pose financial challenges, especially if you're just starting out. Financial planning is the key to maintaining the length and safety of your career.

To do this you have to understand how to budget. With erratic pay cheques, sky-high rent, and crippling student debt, how is anyone meant to do it?

The fact is that as a freelance creative, checking that tax and national insurance, rent and essential bills are paid, stops us ending up in prison – so it *must* be done. As a freelance actor you are *entirely* responsible for yourself in these matters.

Goals and obstacles

Goal
To balance what comes in with what goes out, and pay rent, tax, National Insurance, and essential bills.

Obstacles
The amount that comes in is different every week, month, year (and some of this must be put aside for tax and National Insurance).

Strategies

1. The bill payer

What is it?
If you do not earn enough money from acting to pay the bills, use your dyslexic strengths to earn some more.

Why is it useful?
Actors have many other strengths to share which benefit others and ourselves. Doing so can make you feel good, and, crucially, bring in more money.

How do I do it?
Consider your strengths. You are very likely able to work in some of these areas:
- Retail
- Hospitality
- Corporate/PR/marketing events
- Front of house in a business, on reception
- Entertaining children as a professional clown or party organiser
- Nanny or manny
- Odd jobs person
- Dog-walking
- Tutoring
- Theatre auditorium, box office, or bar staff
- Drama lessons and workshops for young people.

...and many more.

Taking this kind of work is not a failing. Don't think of yourself as an 'out-of-work actor' but as an 'ever-ready actor'!

Think outside the box
Be different to have an impact. Emails go nowhere. They are impersonal and only add to a list for the receiver to plough through, often deleting before reading. So:
- Walk into theatres, bars, restaurants, and other places of work, and talk to people face to face with CV in hand.
- Rehearse a speech: 'I am an actor with some free time. I would really like to be involved in a second career here at... where I can feel part of a team.'

The Dyslexic Actor

- Also type out this information on several pieces of paper, with interesting and relevant detail, plus your email and mobile number, website, or social media handle. Ask for this note to be pinned on the green room board, in the staff room, etc. Make it personal and count. In a theatre, for example, put one in an envelope for the Front of House Manager, one for box office, one for bar staff, etc. Use this personal way to present yourself in technicolour, instead of a dull email.
- Get onto social media with your ideas, and be creative. Post what you are looking to achieve, for example: 'Manny/Nanny available for work/tutoring/entertainment. Are you a parent who needs help with your kids? I'm an actor with great social and communication skills, offering… I would be really pleased to take your kids to the park every afternoon in the school holidays for drama games, exercise, chats… My rate is £… per hour. Direct message me for more info…'
- Be specific and write as if you were writing to a person you know, offering them a bespoke service. Errors are made when you don't hold tight to your intention and follow it through.
- Research tutoring companies who want tutors in drama, music, or any of your other skills, and call them. Pick up the phone and chat: it works.
- Look up children's party entertainment companies. Ring them and ask if they need another entertainer. Find out from them how to get into that business

if you like the idea. Be real and honest and reveal yourself.

Follow-up
Finding a fit for work takes time and sticking to your objective. After visiting or calling, put it in your calendar to call again or visit in two weeks. Too many people ask 'do you have any vacancies?' and the person on the other end of the phone instinctively says 'no'. What you want to do is to make an impact so they want to work with *you*. How can you do this?

2. Hire an accountant

What is it?
So now you have enough funds coming in (whether that be with two or three jobs, universal credit, family help, etc.) Tax and national insurance must be paid. It's a legal obligation to contribute to the pots which fund hospitals, highways, schools and welfare for your country of residence.

Why is it useful?
It stops you being fined and possibly going to prison!

How do I do it?
Register with HMRC as soon as you start receiving an income. Do it within six months of working. This is done online.

As a self-employed person or 'freelancer', you have to

fill out a 'self-assessment tax return' and pay tax by 31st January each year otherwise you are fined.

But don't panic, there are accountants who fill out tax returns for you! Can you believe it? They are qualified to understand what is lawful, and for approximately £250 a year (at time of writing), they will take this problem off your plate.

Some people choose to tackle it themselves. My advice is to hire a specialist first and you can always ask to sit with them after several years and see how it is done.

You can claim reasonable expenses back from the government against what you earn over £12,570 (at time of writing). However, you have to be able to evidence these expenses. So you should keep the receipts for things you have paid for, and also give your accountant all bank statements for the year you are paying tax on. They can see what might be a reasonable expense. Some examples might be:

- Headshots
- Agent's commission
- Union fees (e.g. Equity)
- Spotlight membership
- Rehearsal clothing
- Dance shoes
- Stationery
- Your accountant's fee!

After the reasonable expenses have been deducted, any profit (over £12,570) is taxed at 20%. This means you give the government one fifth of what you earn in tax, but as a freelancer it might be a year before you actually have to pay it, so that 20% must be saved from each payment you are given.

All of the work you do, whether acting or front of house work, tutoring, and so on will be included in the tax calculation.

Some of the work you might do *outside* of acting (the things mentioned in the first strategy, above – from page 273) will be 'PAYE' – this means 'Pay As You Earn'. The employer will take the tax out of what they pay you, so you don't have to worry about saving the extra 20% in that case.

National Insurance
National Insurance also has to be paid. It contributes to central funds for things like statutory maternity leave, statutory sick pay, and the state pension. As a freelance worker, this might be the only pension you receive, so it's important to pay it. You will get it back at some point in your retirement years as a monthly payment.

3. Budgeting

What is it?
Making sure that you can always pay the essential bills you have to pay, and that beyond those, you only spend what you can afford.

Why is it useful?
It stops you getting into debt.

How do I do it?
Set up a 'jam-jar' bank account (research online to find the various options which exist). These allow you to create different compartments within the same account where you put the money you need for different things. Some accounts call them 'pots' or 'spaces'.

When you open the account, enter the details of all the essential bills you pay each month. These might include rent, utilities and council tax bills, mobile phone bills, broadband bills, your Netflix subscription, your Spotlight subscription, credit card payments, and so on.

You should also think about things that you don't actually pay for on a monthly basis but that will be big lump sums at some point in the year.

If your accountant charges £250 per year, perhaps you should include £25 per month to be set aside in your budgeting for that expenditure.

Your tax bill is likely to be the biggest annual payment that you have to save for. Set aside an amount towards this each month as well.

Money for all these regular payments should be set aside in a compartment specially for them – called 'Bills'.

Give the details of this bank account to everyone who pays you.

Your direct debits for all those regular bill payments will go out of this bank account.

Everything left over is available for you to save (in a separate savings account), or to spend.

You don't *have* to do this using a special 'jam-jar account' – you can do it yourself by working out what all your regular payments add up to and setting that money aside manually – but an account that does it for you might be a useful tool.

> **Tips**
> Look for bargains. Shop in the cheaper supermarkets; use store points cards to get money off your shopping and take a look at their weekly deals and discounts; look for mobile phone contracts with family plans or other discounts; buy theatre tickets through discount schemes and companies, etc.

4. Reflect and re-evaluate every three months

What is it?
Taking two hours in your calendar every three months to look at your finances.

Why is it useful?
It allows you to make changes to your plans and budgeting if your income and expenses have changed, and it stops you being hit by any surprises.

How do I do it?
Set aside two hours in your diary every three months.

When the time comes around, look at everything about your financial situation over those last three months. Ask yourself:
- What went well?
- What was challenging?
- How can I overcome these challenges with different behaviour?
- What have I learned?
- What will I do differently next month?
- Is there going to be any change to my expenditure or my income in the next three months that I need to plan for by changing my budget?
- Am I planning my food for the week to save money?
- Am I making impulse purchases or thinking properly about whether I need things?
- Can I save money by giving anything up – for example, takeaways, or smoking?

Write down the answers to these questions in your actor's memory book (see page 269). Alter your behaviour or your budget plan accordingly.

5. Line up a money mentor/accountability buddy

What is it?
This is a bit like the 'Accountability buddy' strategy for organisation on page 236, but you should choose someone particular for this task – a person you trust (with

some knowledge or more experience than you) to offer advice on finances. In return, share some of your own tips that you've learned as you've gone along.

Why is it useful?
Dyslexic people can live in a hidden bubble of shame where their head is in the sand, and if you have worries or uncertainty about your finances which you don't share with anyone, then the uncomfortable feeling lingers much longer and can develop into a danger for your mental health.

How do I do it?
Chat to creative people who may have more experience or knowledge than you about financial stuff, and ask for help. Don't be ashamed! It is endearing, and authentic, to find the words to say 'Can you help me learn about money please?'. People will like and respect you for it.

Pick up the phone, or meet up in person, with a non-judgemental, understanding person who is happy for you to share information and concerns about your finances, in a safe space.

Meet regularly and discuss things until you have a model that seems to work for you. Maybe you will then be able to become that buddy for someone less experienced.

Afterword: Supporting the Dyslexic Actor

Supporting a dyslexic person is hard, because everyone is unique. It's like trying to work out a new gadget that doesn't come with a user manual.

This section is for you if you are:
- An agent
- A parent
- A partner
- A director
- A casting director
- A coach
- A colleague
- A friend

...to someone who is dyslexic.

Why is it useful?
By becoming aware of how your dyslexic person feels, best understands/learns, and navigates daily life, you can help bring out their full potential.

How do I do it?
No matter who you are, or whether you are working individually or in groups, the principles to a lesser or greater extent are the same:
- Acknowledge that the strengths that come with their dyslexic identity are part of what has brought them to the arts.
- Be informed. Read this book! The British Dyslexia Association (**www.bdadyslexia.org.uk**); Patoss (the Professional Association of Teachers of Students with Specific Learning Difficulties – **www.patoss-dyslexia.org**); and PASSHE (The Professional Association of Specific Learning Difference Specialists in Higher Education – formally known as Association of Dyslexia Specialists in Higher Education – **adshe.org.uk**) each offer all kinds of information to help.
- Read about dyslexic brains. There are many examples available online for how a dyslexic individual may see words on the page – a quick search will give you a clear idea of the kind of challenges being dealt with.
- More generally, in the most basic terms, there are four main areas which you need to understand to support learning. The first three often present challenges, while the last is often a strength for dyslexic individuals:

Working memory – the ability to hold on to information in the head for the duration of a task.

Processing speed – how quickly a person can react to information given.

Verbal understanding – how a person understands and processes language, and expresses themselves using it.

Perceptual reasoning – the ability to take a problem and use visual, motor and spatial skills to organise thoughts and create solutions.

If you ask, the dyslexic person can let you know their capabilities and challenges. If I use myself as a simple model for this:
- I can hold on to two or three simple instructions at a time – no more.
- I process information given to me much more slowly than a neurotypical person.
- If I understand information, I express it very well in my own language.
- I think and learn well using my visual and motor skills.

Make the most of the answers you retrieve from the person you are supporting, and try to come up with a model for sharing information or setting tasks that works for them.

- Listen. For a dyslexic person, putting thoughts into words to talk to you can take time, so allow for long pauses. Don't talk over them, finish their sentences, or assume the end of the point they are making.
- Be observant – notice the signs of possible dyslexia. Understand that many people cannot afford or wouldn't think to have an assessment, so they may not know they are dyslexic. Keep an eye out for the

challenges they face, their strengths and, in particular, any disparity between struggles in learning and excelling in other areas. It's a big clue.
- For example, one minute they are captured by an idea: they are all-consumed, enthusiastic, determined, dogged, fully focused, gathering momentum, and speeding forward with force, drive, intensity; unstoppable, excited and positive. The next minute they are:
  o Down-hearted
  o Exhausted
  o Confused
  o Disorientated
  o Disconnected
  o Retracting
  o Masking
  o Needing sleep.
- If this is the case, helping them to identify themselves as being dyslexic is the first step.
- Disclosing being dyslexic takes enormous courage. Denial can also be an unhealthy self-preservation strategy worth looking out for. Offer a safe space where there is no need to pretend. Build trust through listening, encouragement and patience. It is always beneficial to ask 'How can I support you best?'
- Talk about it, and assume nothing – take time to ask curious, interested, open questions and actively listen to the answers.
- Lay out the big picture. If you are making a point or discussing a project, first give a brief overview of the

The Dyslexic Actor

goal or point of the task or activity. Simply, slowly, and clearly. From here, explain in stages: 1, 2, 3. Again, simply. Then the concept will be grasped and the brain engaged. From here, your dyslexic person is on board and can begin to activate their own curiosity and the development of ideas.

- Accept. Whatever the task, they may not be able to do it 'your' way, but they might be very experienced in finding a dyslexic solution to achieve the same outcome. Allow them this re-framing and difference, and encourage it.
- Repeat yourself, to allow processing, and reiterate the goal, the purpose of any activity. BUT...
- Also *demonstrate* what you want from an exercise/task. The more speaking you do, the less they will retain. Much better to model it, let them do it, let them hear it, let them see it – and break it down into one layer at a time. Don't move to the next layer until the individual demonstrates understanding.
- Then ask the dyslexic person to demonstrate or explain back to you – it helps their processing but also ensures there aren't misunderstandings. Link new information to the base of knowledge already understood.
- One thing at a time. Don't speak instructions while the dyslexic actor is 'doing', and risk a clash in processing ability. Speak to them after the action is performed.
- Keep it short. Offer up small chunks of information. Any more than two or three instructions at a time cannot be absorbed.

- Keep it slow. In my experience, dyslexic individuals can need learning time squared in order to achieve the same as a typical learner i.e. 4 hours = 16. However, once they have the gist, the time is made up for you by courage, out-of-the-box thinking and extraordinary results. I must acknowledge, though, that group work can be a challenge if abilities widely differ. If concepts are learned at different speeds, consider break-off groups and buddying partnerships.
- Understand that any alterations to plans already absorbed will need slow re-programming, with time for adjustment. While this extra time might not always be available, you need to be ready for the dyslexic individual to find adjusting a little more difficult. For example, re-blocking a scene which has already been absorbed in the body is not impossible but may require more run-throughs than you would imagine or than other actors may need.
- Remember, a dyslexic person can be a master of deception, having had years of practice at hiding their challenges so you won't think they are stupid. Ask that any confusion is brought up directly and not masked. Explain that if one person is confused, it is likely another is too, and that the information hasn't been explained as best it should be. This is for the benefit of everybody, as if the first layer is not understood, the whole overall concept will not be mastered and faking will occur.
- Offer reasonable adjustment to your methods in whatever you are doing. Colour is often a useful tool.

There are some tips in earlier chapters of this book about adjustments that can be made to, for example, the teaching of choreography (see page 65) or accents (page 42), or the running of auditions (page 167).
- Seek out playful ways of doing things: Think playfully of alternative methods that achieve the same outcome. Does a read-through have to be done sitting down around a table? Movement in the room, in this or any other scenario, may allow the dyslexic actor to think, process and be free. Allowing for play and laughter will keep them feeling relaxed in the space.
- Allow for periods to digest. The dyslexic actor may read aloud well, but not have enough of an idea what they are saying to be able to discuss it straight afterwards – information may not be fully assimilated until the next day. At the very least, ask the dyslexic person their thoughts towards the *end* of a discussion, as it is when hearing other ideas and talking through them that opinions are generally formed.
- More often than not (although not exclusively), a quiet atmosphere is best for line-absorbing. Keeping a dyslexic ensemble member in the rehearsal when lines need to be embedded, may be counter-productive. Allow time at the outset for private learning to be quiet and absorbed out of rehearsal. Bring them back into the ensemble when lines are more embedded, and the results are often much better.
- Offer encouragement. A dyslexic person is only too aware of their years of struggling at school, and of feeling a failure. This is fundamentally a part of them.

An awful lot of self-esteem needs lifting to allow the actor to play freely. If you want your individual to function safely and to the best of their ability, consider your ratio of praise to criticism, and give feedback constructively and face-to-face, with a suggestion about how to correct anything that isn't as you'd like it. Also be careful always to include and notice them. Make the individual feel valued, heard and included.
- Develop an awareness of intersectionality. Having an understanding of how aspects of a person's social and political identity combine to create different privileges, is very helpful. Gender, class, disability, physical appearance, religion, sex and sexuality, etc., can all play their part in this. Take time to acknowledge your own position and that of the dyslexic individual you are working with, and embed this knowledge into your wider understanding of them as a human.

Two final aspects to be aware of:
- Considerations about language: In my opinion a person doesn't 'have' dyslexia (or any other co-occuring neurodivergences). They 'are' dyslexic, or neurodivergent, as it affects every aspect of life in both positive and challenging ways. Dyslexia is a part of the identity, rather than a condition. Dyslexia is best talked about as being 'identified' rather than 'diagnosed'.
- Age and experience makes no difference to whether one is more or less dyslexic. Naturally, if a person is newly out of the education system and the majority

of their life has been those uncomfortable formative years at school, their self-esteem is likely to be low. However, 'compensated' dyslexics are those who have worked with dedication and commitment to re-frame, develop and progress through inherent challenges, to function well in society. Also, while dyslexia is now more commonly identified while a person is in the education system, many older dyslexic people have never been assessed.

As a process, supporting a dyslexic person is not without challenges, but enter their world – see the world differently, and it can be fun, transformative and hugely rewarding.

Acknowledgements

My sincere thanks to:
Matt Applewhite and Nick Hern Books
Sarah Lambie, editor
Jude Tisdall, arts advisor
Lynne Hale, mentor
Rebecca Banatvala, actor and first editor
Sophie Jacob, actor and creative
Jamie Crabb, neurodivergent specialist
Phoebe Stapleton, movement director
Lisa Lapage, voice specialist
Jon Stapleton, director of photography
Daniel-Konrad Cooper, film producer
Sir Richard Eyre – for listening

Accents:
Jade Alexander (Australian)
Conor O'Kane (Northern Irish)
Matt Addis (Welsh)
Colette de Grazia (General American)
David Fairs (Newcastle)

Ellen Newman, voice/acting coach, for the courage to tackle a fear of words, especially Shakespeare; who witnessed, supported and unswervingly encouraged.

The author gratefully acknowledges permission to reproduce extracts from the following plays, all published by Nick Hern Books: *Two Billion Beats* by Sonali Bhattacharyya; *Jerusalem* by Jez Butterworth; *Driftwood* by Tim Foley; *A Sudden Violent Burst of Rain* by Sami Ibrahim; *Imperium: The Cicero Plays*, based on the *Cicero* trilogy by Robert Harris, adapted by Mike Poulton; *Pennyroyal* by Lucy Roslyn; and *Red Pitch* by Tyrell Williams.

More books for actors and creatives from Nick Hern Books

An Actor's Alphabet
An A to Z of Some Stuff I've Learnt and Some Stuff I'm Still Learning
Julie Hesmondhalgh

Advice from the Players
Laura Barnett

An Attitude for Acting
How to Survive (and Thrive) as an Actor
Andrew Tidmarsh and Tara Swart

Developing Your Emotional Health
The Compact Guide
Andy Barker, Brian Cooley & Beth Wood

The Golden Rules of Acting
and **More Golden Rules of Acting**
Andy Nyman

The Jobbing Actor
A Coaching Programme for Actors
Letty Butler & Anita Gilbert

Other People's Shoes
Thoughts on Acting
Harriet Walter

This Book is Short
A Toolkit for Creative ADHDers
Tom Ryalls

The Working Actor
The Essential Guide to a Successful Career
Paul Clayton

Discover more at
www.nickhernbooks.co.uk/acting

www.nickhernbooks.co.uk

@nickhernbooks